15.

THE
OXFORD
Junior
ATLAS

Acknowledgements

The publishers would like to thank the following
for permission to reproduce photographs

AA Photo Library: 37 top right; Aerofilms Limited: 13, 30 all;
Bryan & Cherry Alexander Photography: 58 middle, 61 middle;
Austin Brown/Aviation Picture Library: 66 right;
British Petroleum Shipping Ltd (Fotoflite): 67 right;
Chorley & Handford: 7 all, 32 all, 34;
Comstock Photo Library: 54, 58 bottom left, 59 middle,
60 bottom middle, 61 right;
English Heritage Photographic Library: 37 bottom left;
The Environmental Picture Library: 36, 63 left; FLPA:
60 bottom right;
Greg Evans International; 37 top left, 58 bottom middle,
58 bottom right, 59 bottom left;
Robert Harding Picture Library Ltd: 33 top, 33 middle,
60 top right, 62 top;
Holt Studios International: 31 all;
The Hutchison Library: 33 bottom, 62 bottom;
David Keith Jones/Images of Africa Photobank: 59 bottom right;
Mark Mason: 4 top right, 5;
National Remote Sensing Centre (Airphotogroup): 4 top left;
Marilyn O'Brien: 37 bottom right;
Christine Osborne Pictures: 60 bottom left;
Port of Felixstowe: 67 left; Rex Features: 62 middle;
Science Photo Library: 14, 56 middle, 57, 60 top left, 66 left;
Skyscan: 34 right; Still Pictures: 56 bottom;
The Telegraph Colour Library: 59 bottom middle,
60 top middle, 65;
Tropix Photographic Library: 63 right;
United States Atlantic Fleet Submarine Force:,
Public Affairs Office 55.

Cover image:
Tom Van Sant / Geosphere Project, Santa Monica ,
Science Photo Library.

The illustrations are by Chapman Bounford, Hard Lines,
Mike Harkins, and Gary Hinks.

The page design is by Adrian Smith.

OXFORD
UNIVERSITY PRESS

Great Clarendon Street, Oxford OX2 6DP

Oxford University Press is a department of the University of Oxford.
It furthers the University's objective of excellence in research, scholarship,
and education by publishing worldwide in

Oxford New York

Athens Auckland Bangkok Bogotá Buenos Aires Cape Town
Chennai Dar es Salaam Delhi Florence Hong Kong Istanbul Karachi
Kolkata Kuala Lumpur Madrid Melbourne Mexico City Mumbai Nairobi
Paris São Paulo Shanghai Singapore Taipei Tokyo Toronto Warsaw

with associated companies in Berlin Ibadan

Oxford is a registered trade mark of Oxford University Press
in the UK and in certain other countries

© Oxford University Press 1996

First published 1996
Reprinted 1996, with corrections 1997,
1998 (twice), with corrections 1999, 2000, 2001 (twice)

© Maps copyright Oxford University Press

ISBN 0 19 831793 X (paperback)   ISBN 0 19 831834 0 (hardback)

Printed in Italy by G. Canale & C. S.p.A. - Borgaro T.se - Turin

Editorial Adviser

Patrick Wiegand

Oxford University Press

2 Contents

Atlas information

The British Isles

The United Kingdom

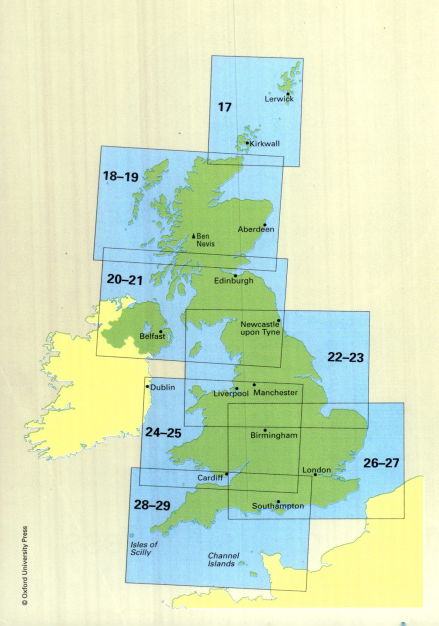

Contents 3

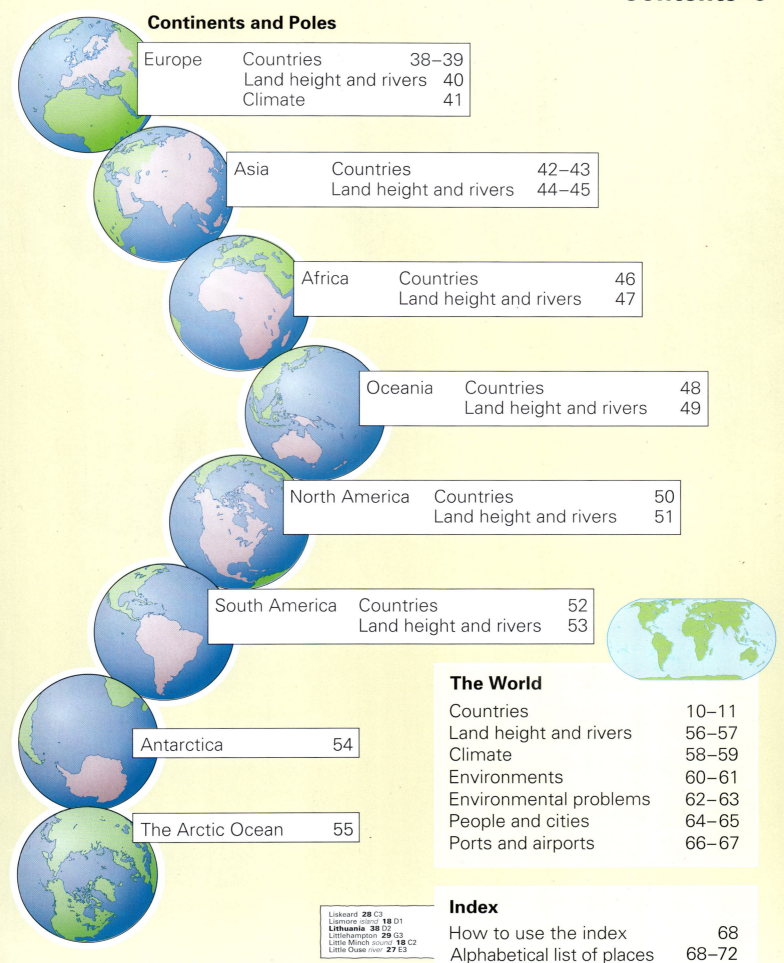

Continents and Poles

The World

Liskeard **28** C3
Lismore *island* **18** D1
Lithuania 38 D2
Littlehampton **29** G3
Little Minch *sound* **18** C2
Little Ouse *river* **27** E3

Index

© Oxford University Press

4 Round Earth

A globe shows the Earth as a sphere.

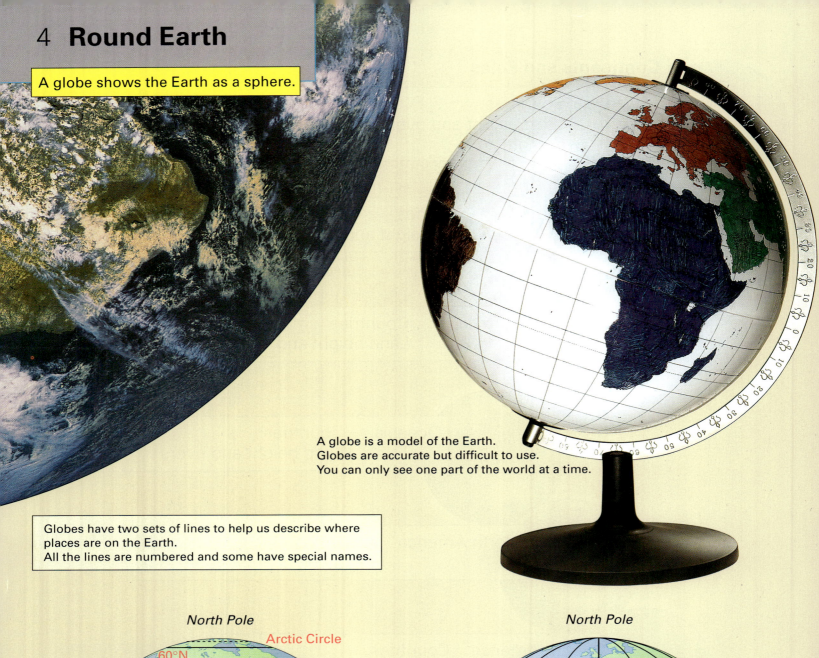

A globe is a model of the Earth.
Globes are accurate but difficult to use.
You can only see one part of the world at a time.

Globes have two sets of lines to help us describe where places are on the Earth.
All the lines are numbered and some have special names.

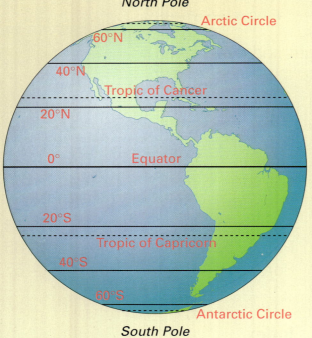

These are lines of latitude.

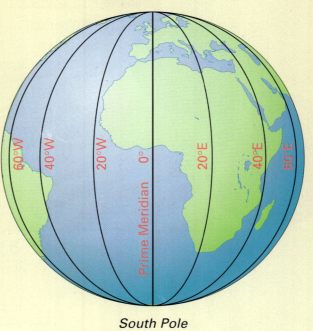

These are lines of longitude.

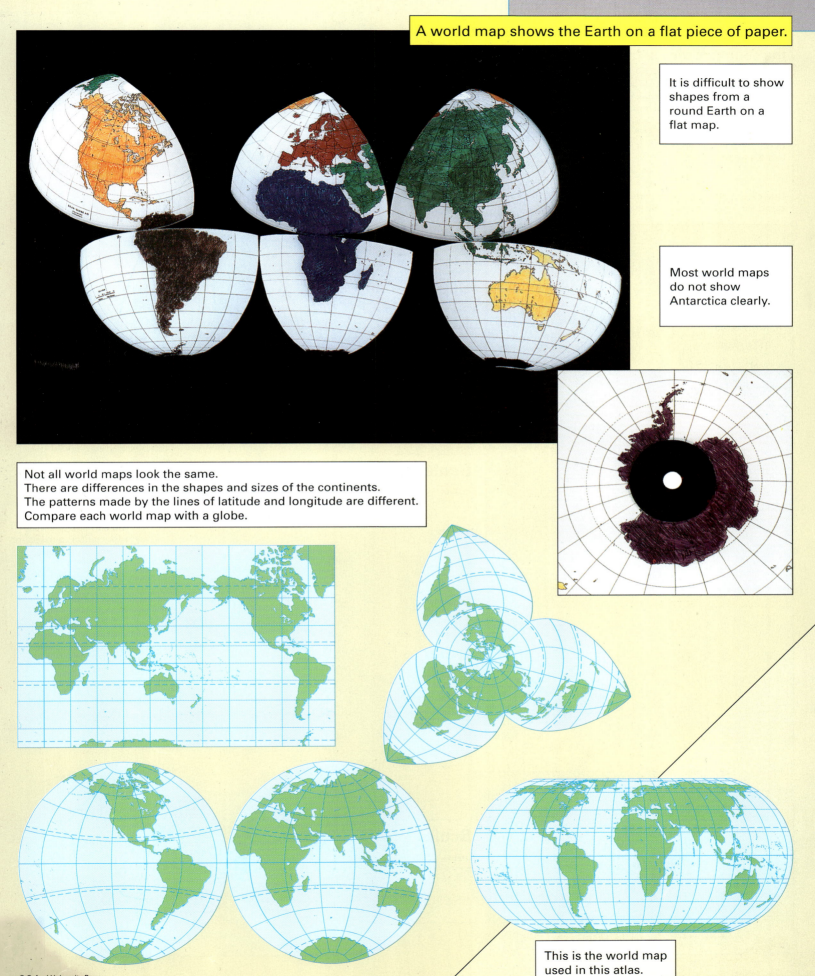

A world map shows the Earth on a flat piece of paper.

It is difficult to show shapes from a round Earth on a flat map.

Most world maps do not show Antarctica clearly.

Not all world maps look the same.
There are differences in the shapes and sizes of the continents.
The patterns made by the lines of latitude and longitude are different.
Compare each world map with a globe.

This is the world map used in this atlas.

6 Scale

One centimetre on a map has to stand for many kilometres on the ground.

Every map in this atlas has a sign like this :

12 km →
one cm

One centimetre on a map with *this* sign would stand for 12 kilometres on the ground.

You can see more detail on some maps than others. The amount of detail depends on the **scale** of the map.
See how the British Isles become smaller as the scale changes on the maps below.

Scale

20 km →
one cm

Scale

100 km →
one cm

Scale

1000 km →
one cm

Scale

2000 km →
one cm

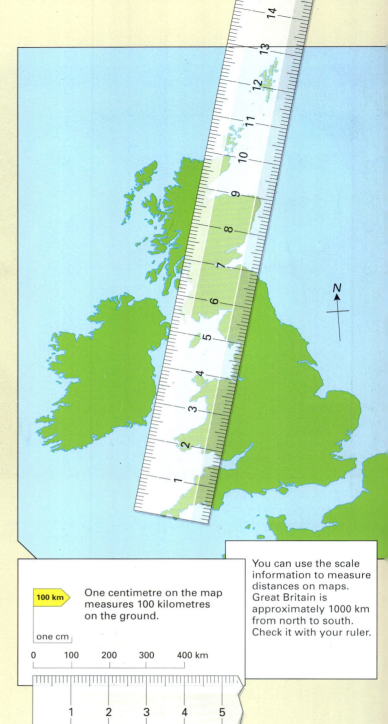

N

100 km →
one cm

One centimetre on the map measures 100 kilometres on the ground.

0   100   200   300   400 km

1   2   3   4   5

You can use the scale information to measure distances on maps. Great Britain is approximately 1000 km from north to south. Check it with your ruler.

Small maps like this on some pages of the atlas help you to compare the size of other countries with the British Isles.

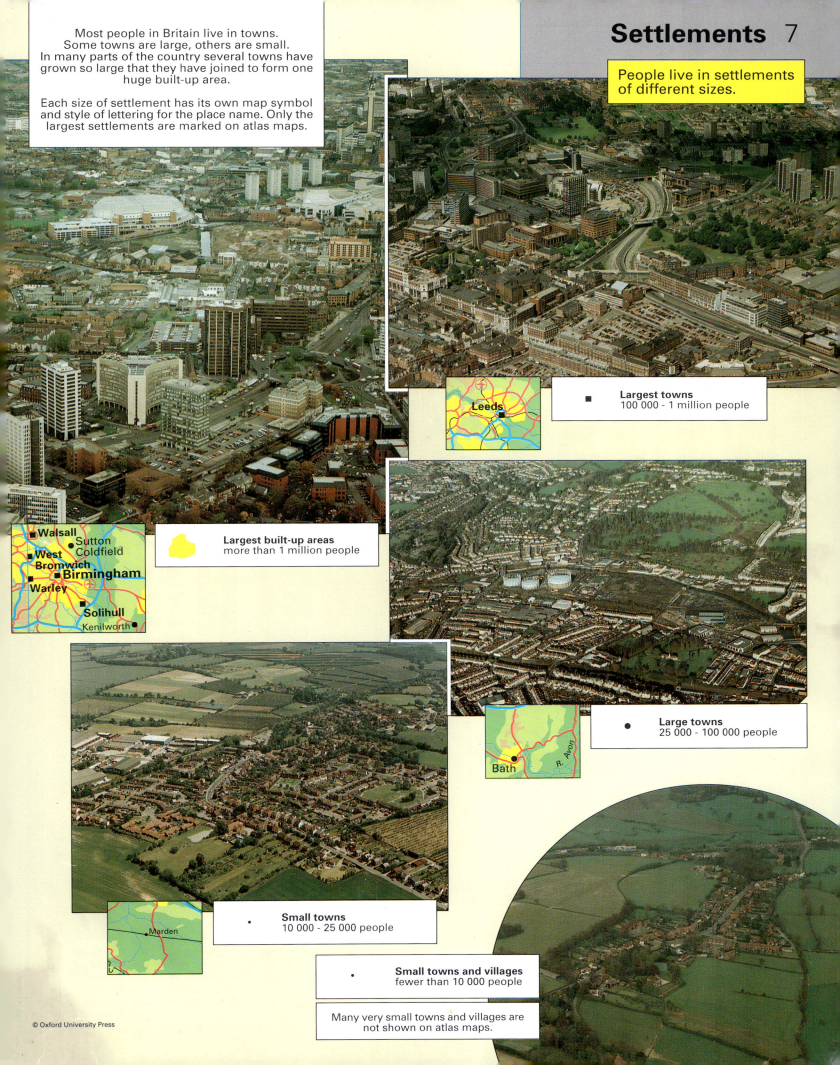

Most people in Britain live in towns.
Some towns are large, others are small.
In many parts of the country several towns have grown so large that they have joined to form one huge built-up area.

Each size of settlement has its own map symbol and style of lettering for the place name. Only the largest settlements are marked on atlas maps.

People live in settlements of different sizes.

Largest towns
100 000 - 1 million people

Leeds

Largest built-up areas
more than 1 million people

Walsall
Sutton Coldfield
West Bromwich
Birmingham
Warley
Solihull
Kenilworth

Large towns
25 000 - 100 000 people

Bath
R. Avon

Small towns
10 000 - 25 000 people

Marden

Small towns and villages
fewer than 10 000 people

Many very small towns and villages are not shown on atlas maps.

© Oxford University Press

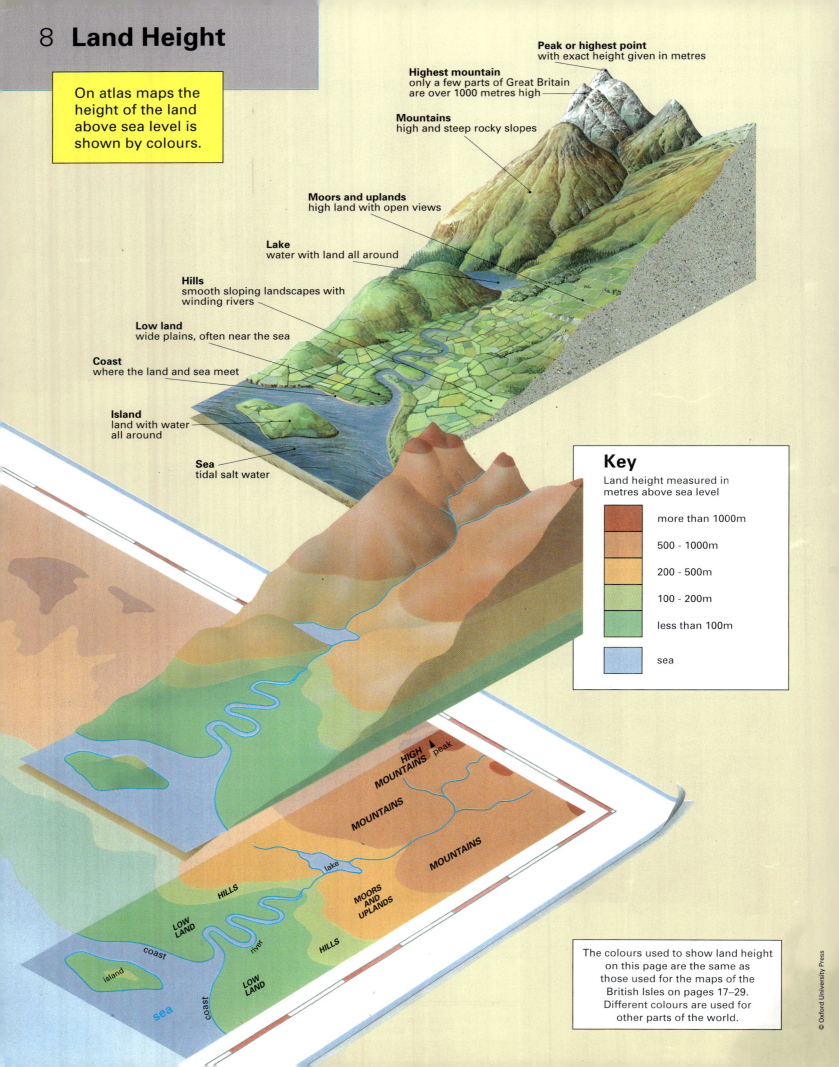

On atlas maps the height of the land above sea level is shown by colours.

Peak or highest point
with exact height given in metres

Highest mountain
only a few parts of Great Britain
are over 1000 metres high

Mountains
high and steep rocky slopes

Moors and uplands
high land with open views

Lake
water with land all around

Hills
smooth sloping landscapes with
winding rivers

Low land
wide plains, often near the sea

Coast
where the land and sea meet

Island
land with water
all around

Sea
tidal salt water

Key

Land height measured in
metres above sea level

more than 1000m

500 - 1000m

200 - 500m

100 - 200m

less than 100m

sea

HIGH MOUNTAINS peak

MOUNTAINS

MOUNTAINS

MOORS AND UPLANDS

lake

HILLS

HILLS

LOW LAND

river

coast

LOW LAND

island

coast

sea

The colours used to show land height
on this page are the same as
those used for the maps of the
British Isles on pages 17–29.
Different colours are used for
other parts of the world.

© Oxford University Press

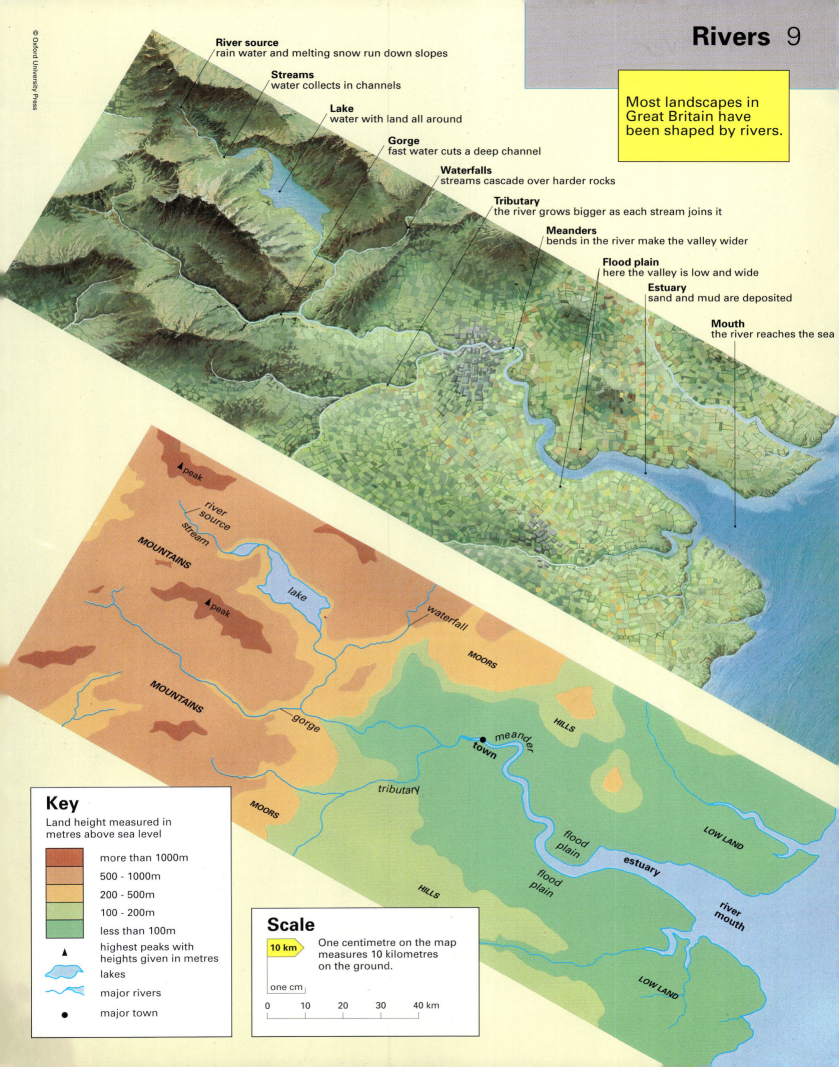

© Oxford University Press

River source
rain water and melting snow run down slopes

Streams
water collects in channels

Lake
water with land all around

Gorge
fast water cuts a deep channel

Waterfalls
streams cascade over harder rocks

Tributary
the river grows bigger as each stream joins it

Meanders
bends in the river make the valley wider

Flood plain
here the valley is low and wide

Estuary
sand and mud are deposited

Mouth
the river reaches the sea

Most landscapes in Great Britain have been shaped by rivers.

peak

river source

stream

MOUNTAINS

peak

lake

waterfall

MOORS

MOUNTAINS

gorge

HILLS

meander

town

tributary

MOORS

HILLS

flood plain

flood plain

estuary

LOW LAND

river mouth

LOW LAND

Key

Land height measured in
metres above sea level

more than 1000m

500 - 1000m

200 - 500m

100 - 200m

less than 100m

▲ highest peaks with
heights given in metres

lakes

major rivers

● major town

Scale

10 km ▶ One centimetre on the map
measures 10 kilometres
on the ground.

one cm

0   10   20   30   40 km

A country is a land with its own people and its own laws.

Scale

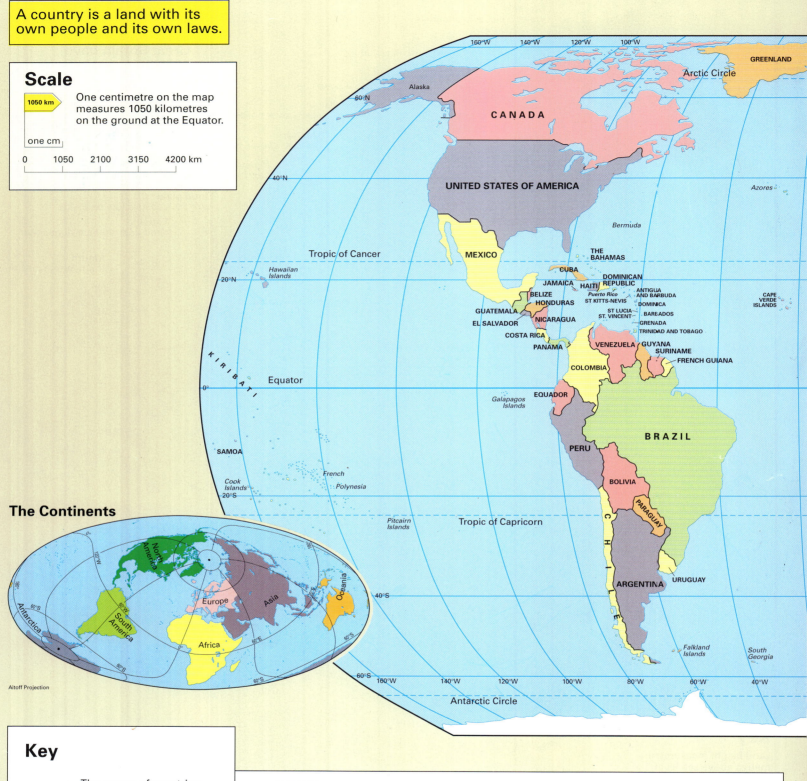

1050 km

One centimetre on the map measures 1050 kilometres on the ground at the Equator.

one cm

| 0 | 1050 | 2100 | 3150 | 4200 km |

The Continents

Aitoff Projection

Key

CANADA — The names of countries are shown with this type of lettering.

Countries that are too small to be named on the map are shown by the first few letters of their name.

 These colours are used to show where one country ends and another begins.

A	ALBANIA	CZ	CZECH REPUBLIC	N	NETHERLANDS
AR	ARMENIA	F	FYROM (FORMER YUGOSLAV REPUBLIC OF MACEDONIA)	Q	QATAR
AU	AUSTRIA			R	ROMANIA
AZ	AZERBAIJAN			S	SLOVAKIA
B	BELGIUM	G	THE GAMBIA	SL	SLOVENIA
BD	BRUNEI DARUSSALAM	G-B	GUINEA-BISSAU	SW	SWITZERLAND
BE	BENIN	H	HUNGARY	T	TAJIKISTAN
BH	BOSNIA-HERZEGOVINA	IS	ISRAEL	TU	TURKMENISTAN
BU	BURKINA	L	LEBANON	U	UGANDA
C	CROATIA	LI	LITHUANIA	UAE	UNITED ARAB EMIRATES
CAR	CENTRAL AFRICAN REPUBLIC	LU	LUXEMBOURG	Y	YUGOSLAVIA
				ZIM	ZIMBABWE

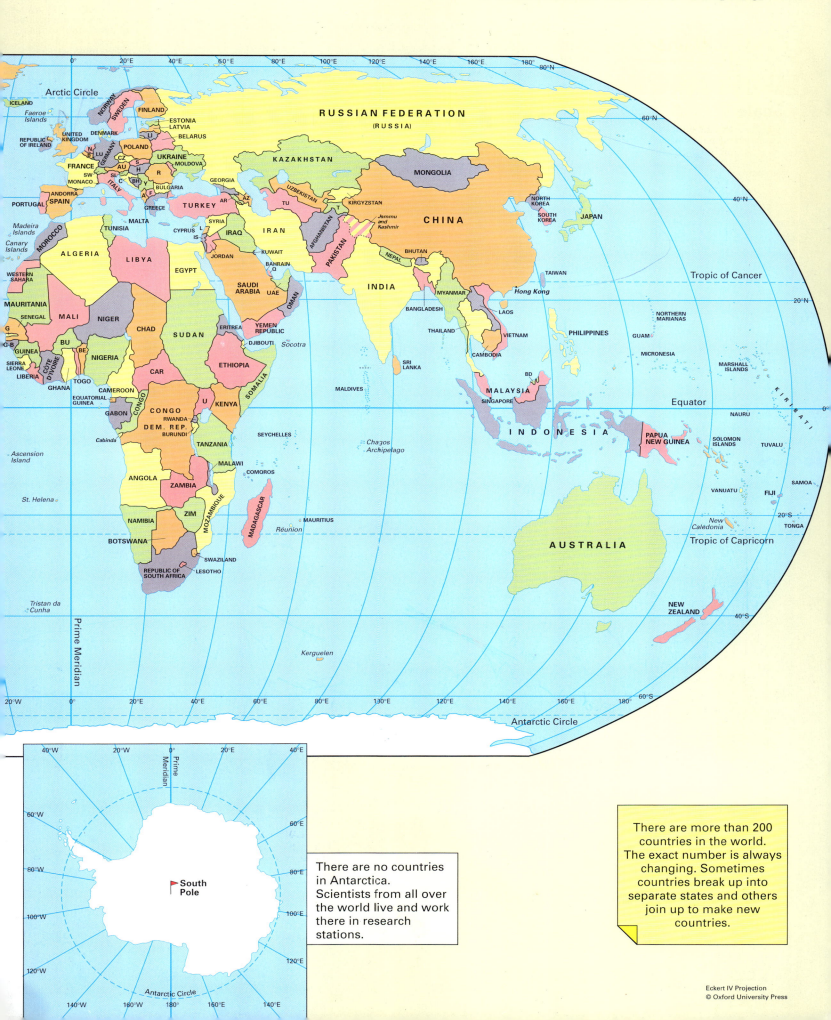

Arctic Circle

ICELAND

Faeroe
Islands

NORWAY SWEDEN FINLAND

REPUBLIC
OF IRELAND

UNITED
KINGDOM DENMARK ESTONIA
LATVIA

N LU GERMANY POLAND BELARUS

FRANCE B CZ UKRAINE

SW AU H R MOLDOVA

SL C BH Y

MONACO SI F BULGARIA

ANDORRA ITALY GEORGIA

PORTUGAL SPAIN GREECE TURKEY AR AZ

Madeira
Islands TUNISIA MALTA CYPRUS L SYRIA

Canary
Islands MOROCCO IS IRAQ IRAN

RUSSIAN FEDERATION
(RUSSIA)

KAZAKHSTAN

MONGOLIA

UZBEKISTAN

KIRGYZSTAN

TU T

Jammu
and
Kashmir

CHINA

NORTH
KOREA

SOUTH
KOREA

JAPAN

ALGERIA LIBYA EGYPT JORDAN KUWAIT AFGHANISTAN PAKISTAN NEPAL BHUTAN

WESTERN
SAHARA SAUDI
ARABIA BAHRAIN
Q UAE OMAN INDIA MYANMAR

MAURITANIA SENEGAL MALI NIGER CHAD SUDAN ERITREA YEMEN
REPUBLIC DJIBOUTI Socotra

G GUINEA BU BE NIGERIA CAR ETHIOPIA SOMALIA

G-B SIERRA
LEONE LIBERIA CÔTE
D'IVOIRE GHANA TOGO CAMEROON

EQUATORIAL
GUINEA GABON CONGO DEM. REP. CONGO U RWANDA BURUNDI KENYA

Cabinda TANZANIA

Ascension
Island SEYCHELLES

St. Helena ANGOLA ZAMBIA MALAWI COMOROS

NAMIBIA ZIM MOZAMBIQUE MADAGASCAR Réunion MAURITIUS

BOTSWANA

SWAZILAND

REPUBLIC OF
SOUTH AFRICA LESOTHO

Tristan da
Cunha

Kerguelen

Tropic of Cancer

TAIWAN

Hong Kong

BANGLADESH LAOS

THAILAND VIETNAM PHILIPPINES

CAMBODIA

SRI
LANKA

MALDIVES

Chagos
Archipelago

BD

MALAYSIA

SINGAPORE

INDONESIA

Equator

PAPUA
NEW GUINEA

NORTHERN
MARIANAS

GUAM

MICRONESIA

MARSHALL
ISLANDS

K I R I B A T I

NAURU

SOLOMON
ISLANDS TUVALU

SAMOA

VANUATU FIJI

New
Caledonia TONGA

AUSTRALIA

Tropic of Capricorn

NEW
ZEALAND

Antarctic Circle

Prime Meridian

There are no countries
in Antarctica.
Scientists from all over
the world live and work
there in research
stations.

South
Pole

Prime
Meridian

There are more than 200
countries in the world.
The exact number is always
changing. Sometimes
countries break up into
separate states and others
join up to make new
countries.

Eckert IV Projection
© Oxford University Press

England, Scotland, and Wales, together with Northern Ireland, form the United Kingdom. The Republic of Ireland is a separate country.

England is divided into counties and some new unitary authorities. Wales and Scotland are divided into unitary authorities. Northern Ireland is divided into districts.

The Republic of Ireland is divided into counties.

Scale

45 km

One centimetre on the map measures 45 kilometres on the ground

one cm

0   45   90   135   180 km

Key to districts in Northern Ireland

1 Belfast
2 Newtownabbey
3 Carrickfergus
4 Castlereagh
5 North Down
6 Ards
7 Down
8 Newry & Mourne
9 Banbridge
10 Lisburn
11 Craigavon
12 Armagh
13 Dungannon
14 Fermanagh
15 Omagh
16 Cookstown
17 Magherafelt
18 Strabane
19 Londonderry
20 Limavady
21 Coleraine
22 Ballymoney
23 Moyle
24 Ballymena
25 Larne
26 Antrim

Key to unitary authorities in Scotland

1 West Dunbartonshire
2 East Dunbartonshire
3 North Lanarkshire
4 Glasgow City
5 East Renfrewshire
6 Renfrewshire
7 Inverclyde
8 Clackmannanshire
9 Falkirk
10 West Lothian
11 City of Edinburgh
12 Midlothian
13 East Lothian
14 North Ayrshire
15 East Ayrshire
16 Dundee City

Key to unitary authorities in Wales

1 Cardiff
2 The Vale of Glamorgan
3 Bridgend
4 Swansea
5 Neath Port Talbot
6 Rhondda Cynon Taff
7 Merthyr Tydfil
8 Caerphilly
9 Blaenau Gwent
10 Monmouthshire
11 Conwy
12 Denbighshire
13 Flintshire
14 Wrexham

Key to unitary authorities in England

1 Hartlepool
2 Stockton-on-Tees
3 Middlesbrough
4 Redcar and Cleveland
5 East Riding of Yorkshire
6 City of Kingston upon Hull
7 North Lincolnshire
8 North East Lincolnshire
9 South Gloucestershire
10 Bristol
11 North Somerset
12 Bath and North East Somerset
13 Luton
14 Milton Keynes
15 Leicester City
16 Swindon
17 Windsor & Maidenhead

The British Isles consists of the two large islands of Great Britain and Ireland and a number of smaller islands.

Republic of Ireland

United Kingdom

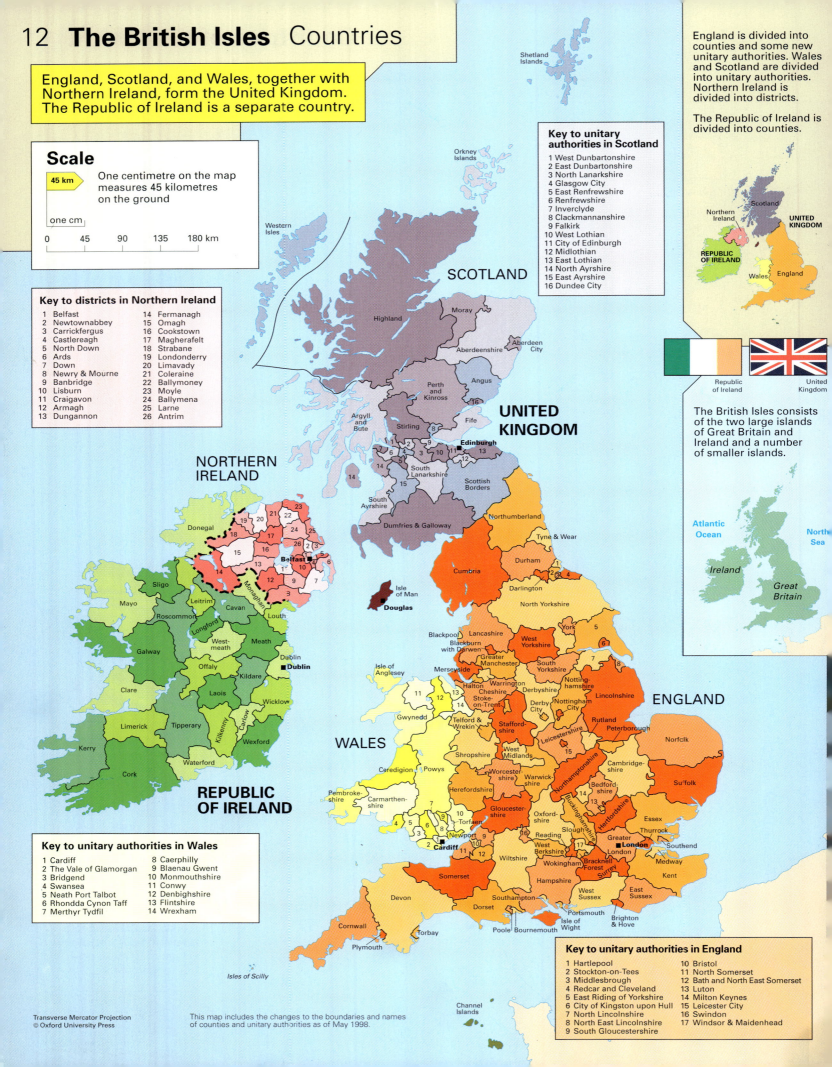

Transverse Mercator Projection
© Oxford University Press

This map includes the changes to the boundaries and names of counties and unitary authorities as of May 1998.

The highest parts of Great Britain are mostly in the north and west.

Scale

45 km One centimetre on the map measures 45 kilometres on the ground.

one cm

| 0 | 45 | 90 | 135 | 180 km |

Key

Land height measured in metres above sea level

- more than 1000m
- 500 - 1000m
- 200 - 500m
- 100 - 200m
- less than 100m
- ▲ highest peaks with heights given in metres
- lakes
- major rivers

1344m ▲ Ben Nevis

The highest mountain in Great Britain is Ben Nevis (1344 metres or 4406 feet high) and the longest river is the Severn (354 kilometres or 220 miles long).

Transverse Mercator Projection
© Oxford University Press

Climate describes the average pattern of weather over a number of years.

During the year many wet weather bands pass over the British Isles whilst southern Europe stays dry and warm. This is a satellite picture of the weather in western Europe on 6 August 1987. Satellite pictures like this use colours that are different from the way the land looks to us.

Transverse Mercator Projection
© Oxford University Press

Rainfall

The eastern parts of the British Isles are drier than the western parts. Mountains are wetter than lowlands.

Valentia •

London

Average annual rainfall in millimetres

	over 2400	very wet
	1500 - 2400	quite wet
	800 - 1500	wet
	600 - 800	quite dry
	less than 600	very dry

Average annual rainfall

The graphs show the amount of rainfall in Valentia and London for one year. Valentia is wetter in winter. London has about the same amount of rainfall each month.

All the rain that falls in one year is the **annual rainfall**. Valentia has much more rain than London over the whole year.

Some years are wetter than others. The map shows the amount of rainfall you would expect in an average year.

Valentia

Amount of rainfall in millimetres

J F M A M J J A S O N D

Months of the year

London

Amount of rainfall in millimetres

J F M A M J J A S O N D

Months of the year

January temperatures

In winter the mountains of
Scotland are the coldest parts
of the British Isles.

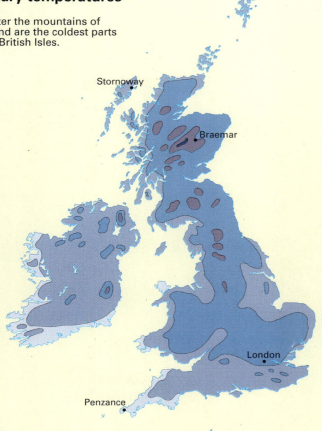

July temperatures

In summer the coasts of southern
England are the warmest parts of
the British Isles.

Scale

100 km

One centimetre on the map
measures 100 kilometres
on the ground.

one cm

0   100   200   300   400 km

Average temperatures in °Celsius

above 16	hot
14 - 16	very warm
12 - 14	warm
10 - 12	quite warm
8 - 10	quite cool
6 - 8	cool
4 - 6	quite cold
2 - 4	cold
0 - 2	very cold
below 0	freezing

In the British Isles
it is usually colder
in January than in July.
However, some years
might be very cold
whilst others are quite warm.
The maps show the
temperatures you would
expect in an average year.

Average temperatures in winter and summer

The graphs show the average
temperatures each month for
Stornoway, Braemar, London,
and Penzance.
In all four places
it is warmer in summer
than in winter.

Summers in Stornoway and
Braemar are much
cooler than in
London or Penzance.
Winter in Braemar is very cold.

Stornoway

temperature in degrees Celsius

Months of the year

Braemar

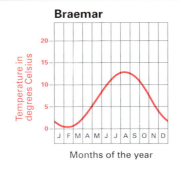

temperature in degrees Celsius

Months of the year

London

temperature in degrees Celsius

Months of the year

Penzance

temperature in degrees Celsius

Months of the year

Transverse Mercator Projection
© Oxford University Press

Maps that show all the most important features of the landscape are called **topographic** maps.

Key

- – – – – – international boundary
- ────── national boundary
- ══════ motorways and main roads
- ────── railway
- ⊕ main airport
- 〜〜〜 river
- 🔵 lake
- ▲ peak or highest point

towns

- 🟡 largest built-up areas
- ■ largest towns
- ● large towns
- · other towns

Scale

45 km ▷ One centimetre on the map measures 45 kilometres on the ground.

one cm

0	45	90	135	180 km

Land height
measured above sea level

- more than 1000m
- 500 – 1000m
- 200 – 500m
- 100 – 200m
- less than 100m

60°N · 58°N · 56°N · 54°N · 52°N · 50°N

Shetland Islands

Orkney Islands

Cape Wrath

NORTHWEST HIGHLANDS

Outer Hebrides

Lewis

Skye

Mull

Islay

Inverness
Great Glen
Loch Ness
River Spey
CAIRNGORMS
1344m ▲
Ben Nevis
GRAMPIAN MOUNTAINS
River Dee
Aberdeen ■
R. Tay
Dundee ■
SCOTLAND
Loch Lomond
Glasgow 🟡
River Clyde
Edinburgh ■
Firth of Forth
Ayr ●
R. Tweed
Firth of Clyde
SOUTHERN UPLANDS
Stranraer ·
CHEVIOT HILLS

UNITED KINGDOM

NORTHERN IRELAND

Coleraine
R. Bann
Londonderry ●
ANTRIM MOUNTAINS
Larne
Lough Neagh
River Erne
Belfast ■
Sligo ·
Carlisle ·
Newcastle upon Tyne
River Tyne
Sunderland ■
LAKE DISTRICT
978m ▲
Scafell Pike
River Eden
River Tees
Middlesbrough ■
NORTH YORK MOORS
River Ouse
PENNINES
Bradford ■ Leeds ■
River Aire
Kingston-upon-Hull ■

North Channel

Isle of Man

Irish Sea

REPUBLIC OF IRELAND

Lough Corrib

Galway ·

River Shannon

R. Boyne

R. Liffey

Dublin ⊕

WICKLOW MOUNTAINS

852m ▲
Slieve Donard

Tiree ·

1041m ▲
Carrauntoohill

Cork ●

River Blackwater

River Suir

Barrow

River

Rosslare ·

St George's Channel

Fishguard ·

ATLANTIC OCEAN

Anglesey
Holyhead ·
Liverpool
Manchester 🟡
River Mersey
Sheffield ■
ENGLAND
Nottingham ●
THE FENS
R. Wensum
Norwich ●
R. Great Ouse

1085m ▲
Snowdon
CAMBRIAN MOUNTAINS
R. Dee
R. Trent
Leicester ●
The Wash

Cardigan Bay

WALES

River Teifi
River Tywi
BRECON BEACONS
River Usk
R. Wye
River Severn
Wolverhampton ■
Birmingham 🟡
River Avon
Northampton ·
R. Stour
Luton ·
CHILTERN HILLS

Swansea ■ Newport ■
Cardiff ■
Bristol Channel
Bristol ■
COTSWOLD HILLS
Oxford ●
R. Thames
Reading ●
London 🟡
Southend-on-Sea ·
Margate ·

EXMOOR
R. Exe
DARTMOOR
Exeter ●
Plymouth ●
Land's End
Penzance ·
Isles of Scilly

SALISBURY PLAIN
Southampton ●
Bournemouth ●
Weymouth ·
Isle of Wight
Portsmouth ■ Brighton ●
SOUTH DOWNS
NORTH DOWNS
Dover ·
Strait of Dover
Calais ■
Boulogne-sur-Mer ■

Bristol Channel

English Channel

North Sea

Prime Meridian

FRANCE
Cherbourg ·
le Havre ■
Rouen ■
R. Seine
Channel Islands ⊕

Scale

10 km

One centimetre on the map measures 10 kilometres on the ground.

one cm

0   10   20   30   40 km

Key

- – – – – county or region boundary
- ━━━━━ motorway and main roads
- ─── railway
- ⊕ main airport
- ─── river
- lake
- ▲ peak or highest point

towns

- • other towns

Land height

measured above sea level

- 200-500m
- 100-200m
- less than 100m

ATLANTIC OCEAN

Herma Ness

Haroldswick

Unst

Point of Fethaland

Yell Sound

Yell

Fetlar

▲ 449m

Esha Ness

Fora Ness

Out Skerries

St Magnus Bay

Muckle Roe

Whalsay

Papa Stour

Symbister

Mainland

SHETLAND ISLANDS

Walls

Bressay

The Deeps

Lerwick

417m

Scalloway

Foula

Sumburgh Head

60°N

60°N

4°W

Fair Isle

Mull Head

Papa Westray

North Ronaldsay

Westray

Sanday

Westray Firth

Rousay

Brough Head

Eday

Stronsay

Stronsay Firth

Shapinsay

Kirkwall

59°N

Stromness

Mainland

ORKNEY ISLANDS

59°N

Scapa

Ward Hill 479m ▲

Scapa Flow

Rora Head

Hoy

South Ronaldsay

North Sea

Pentland Firth

Stroma

Dunnet Head

Strathy Point

John o' Groats

Duncansby Head

Thurso

Halkirk

Kirkwall

Transverse Mercator Projection
© Oxford University Press

4°W   3°W   2°W   1°W

Scale

10 km One centimetre on the map measures 10 kilometres on the ground.

one cm

0 10 20 30 40 km

Key

	county or region boundary
	motorway and main roads
	railway
⊕	main airport
	river
	canal
	lake
▲	peak or highest point

towns

	built-up areas
■	largest towns
●	large towns
•	other towns

Land height

measured above sea level

	more than 1000m
	500-1000m
	200-500m
	100-200m
	less than 100m

ATLANTIC OCEAN

58°N

57°N

8°W

7°W

6°W

St Kilda

Hebrides

Lewis
Stornoway
Broad Bay
EYE PENINSULA

WESTERN ISLES

Scarp

Clisham 799m ▲

Taransay
Tarbert
Harris
Scalpay
Shiant Islands

Outer

Pabbay
Berneray
Sound of Harris

North Uist   Lochmaddy

Benbecula

South Uist

Barra
Castlebay

Eriskay

Mingulay

Little Minch

Rubha Hunish
Kilmaluag

Loch Snizort
The Storr 719m ▲

Dunvegan
Portree
Raasay

Skye
Scalpay
Kyle of Lochalsh

CUILLIN HILLS
Broadford

Soay
Elgol

Calligarry

Inner

Hebrides

Canna

Kinloch
Rhum
Mallaig
Arisaig
Eigg
Sound of Arisaig
Muck

Coll

Tobermory
Lochaline
Sound of Mull

Tiree

Ulva
Craignure
Lismore

Ben More 967m ▲
Mull
Lochdon
Oban
Kerrera

Iona
Fionnphort
ROSS OF MULL

Scarba

Eddrachilli Bay
Enard Bay

The Minch

Ullapoo

Poolewe
Gairloch
Loch Maree

Loch Torridon

Inner Sound

HIGH

River Shiel

Loch Arka

Loch Shiel
Loch Linnhe

Loch Etive

11
Ben Cruach

ARGYL

Furnace

Loch Awe

Firth of Lorn

NORTHW

North
Sea

5°W
4°W
3°W
2°W

E   F   G   H   3   2   1   58   57

Cape Wrath
Head
Strathy Point
John o' Groats
Thurso
Halkirk
Wick
Ben Hope 927m
Lybster
HIGHLANDS
Loch Eriboll
Loch nan Clar
River Thurso
Kinbrace
Morven 705m
River Helmsdale
961m Ben Klibreck
847m Canisp
998m Ben More Assynt
Loch Shin
Helmsdale
Lairg
Brora
Bonar Bridge
Dornoch
Dornoch Firth
Tarbat Ness
Beinn Dearg 1081m
Tain
1109m Sgurr Mór
Invergordon
Cromarty Firth
Cromarty
Moray Firth
Branderburgh
Lossiemouth
Portknockie
Portsoy
Banff
Rosehearty
Fraserburgh
Burghead
Buckie
Cullen
Macduff
1046m Ben Wyvis
Dingwall
Forres
Elgin
R. Spey
Fochabers
Aberchirder
Turriff
Peterhead
Buchan Ness
Nairn
Rothes
Keith
River Deveron
River Meig
N D
R. Beauly
Inverness
Charlestown of Aberlour
Huntly
Oldmeldrum
Ellon
Loch Mullardoch
River Nairn
Grantown-on-Spey
Dufftown
Inverurie
arn Eige 183m
River Spey
MORAY
River Don
ABERDEENSHIRE
River Don
Dyce
ABERDEEN CITY
Aberdeen
Loch Ness
Drumnadrochit
Invermoriston
Aviemore
CAIRNGORMS
Aboyne
River Dee
Fort Augustus
MONADHLIATH MOUNTAINS
Kingussie
Newtonmore
1244m Cairn Gorm
Ballater
Banchory
Invergarry
Braemar
Stonehaven
rt William 1344m Ben Nevis
Ben Alder 1148m
Loch Ericht
G R A M P I A N   M O U N T A I N S
1155m Lochnagar
River North Esk
Laurencekirk
Inverbervie
Loch Lochy
Blackwater Reservoir
PERTH AND KINROSS
River Isla
ANGUS
Milton Ness
Loch Rannoch
Pitlochry
Kirriemuir
River South Esk
Brechin
Montrose
Ben Lawers 1214m
River Tay
Aberfeldy
Blairgowrie
Rattray
Alyth
Forfar
Arbroath
Loch Tay
Tyndrum
Crianlarich
Ben More 1174m
Coupar Angus
SIDLAW HILLS
Carnoustie
Dalmally
Crieff
River Earn
Perth
DUNDEE CITY
Dundee
Firth of Tay
Loch Katrine
Auchterarder
Newburgh
St Andrews
Cupar
Crail
SCOTLAND
ND BUTE
Loch Earn
Callander
OCHIL HILLS
Auchtermuchty
FIFE
Anstruther
nveraray
Tarbet
Ben Lomond 974m
STIRLING
Dunblane
CLACKMANNAN-SHIRE
Glenrothes
Buckhaven
Loch Lomond
River Forth
Stirling
Alloa
Loch Leven
Kinross
Kirkcaldy
Ben Nevis
Aberdeen

Transverse Mercator Projection
© Oxford University Press

Key

‐··‐··‐	international boundary
‐ ‐ ‐	national boundary
‐·‐·‐	county or region boundary
	motorway and main roads
	railway
⊕	main airport
	river
	canal
	lake
▲	peak or highest point

towns

	built-up areas
■	largest towns
●	large towns
·	other towns

Land height

measured above sea level

	more than 1000m
	500-1000m
	200-500m
	100-200m
	less than 100m

Transverse Mercator Projection
© Oxford University Press

Transverse Mercator Projection
© Oxford University Press

Scale

10 km

One centimetre on the map measures 10 kilometres on the ground.

one cm

0   10   20   30   40 km

Scale

10 km▶ One centimetre on the map measures 10 kilometres on the ground

one cm

0 10 20 30 40 km

Key

– – –	national boundary
– – –	county or region boundary
	motorway and main roads
	railway
⊕	main airport
	river
	canal
	lake
▲	peak or highest point

towns

	built-up areas
■	largest towns
●	large towns
·	other towns

Land height

measured above sea level

	more than 1000m
	500-1000m
	200-500m
	100-200m
	less than 100m
	below sea level

Transverse Mercator Projection
© Oxford University Press

Whitley Bay
Tynemouth
North Shields
South Shields
'NE AND WEAR
Sunderland

Peterlee

Hartlepool
HARTLEPOOL
ockton-on-Tees
Middlesbrough
Redcar
OCKTON-TEES
MIDDLESBROUGH
Guisborough
Thornaby-on-Tees
REDCAR AND CLEVELAND
R. Tees

CLEVELAND HILLS

NORTH YORK MOORS

Whitby

River Esk

Northallerton

NORTH YORKSHIRE

Thirsk

Pickering

Scarborough

VALE OF PICKERING

VALE OF YORK

Malton

Norton

YORKSHIRE WOLDS

Great Driffield

Flamborough Head

Bridlington

knaresborough

York
YORK

Wetherby

Tadcaster

EAST RIDING OF YORKSHIRE

River Derwent

River Hull

Hornsea

Selby

River Ouse

Beverley

Castleford

CITY OF KINGSTON UPON HULL
Kingston upon Hull

M62
Pontefract

Goole

NORTH LINCOLNSHIRE

Barton-upon-Humber

River Humber

HOLDERNESS

akefield

Hemsworth

Scunthorpe

Immingham

Barnsley

Brigg

Grimsby

Spurn Head

Doncaster

M180

NORTH EAST LINCOLNSHIRE

Cleethorpes

SOUTH ORKSHIRE

R. Don

Rotherham

R. Trent

Gainsborough

LINCOLN WOLDS

Sheffield

Market Rasen

Louth

Mablethorpe

Worksop

Chesterfield

NOTTINGHAMSHIRE

Lincoln

Horncastle

Spilsby

Skegness

Mansfield

LINCOLNSHIRE

Sutton in Ashfield

River Trent

Newark-on-Trent

River Witham

NOTTINGHAM CITY
Arnold
Nottingham

Grantham

Sleaford

Boston

eston

Derby

Long Eaton

ENGLAND

Melton Mowbray

Spalding

The Wash

Hunstanton

Wells-next-the-Sea

Sheringham
Cromer

Loughborough

R. Soar

R. Great Ouse

THE FENS

King's Lynn

River Bure

Fakenham

NORFOLK BROADS

oalville

LEICESTERSHIRE

RUTLAND

Stamford

Wisbech

R. Great Ouse

R. Nene

Swaffham

NORFOLK

East Dereham

Norwich

Great Yarmouth

LEIC CITY
Leicester
Wigston

Rutland Water

PETERBOROUGH

Peterborough

Downham Market

Wymondham

North Sea

United Kingdom inset:
Newcastle upon Tyne
Manchester
Liverpool

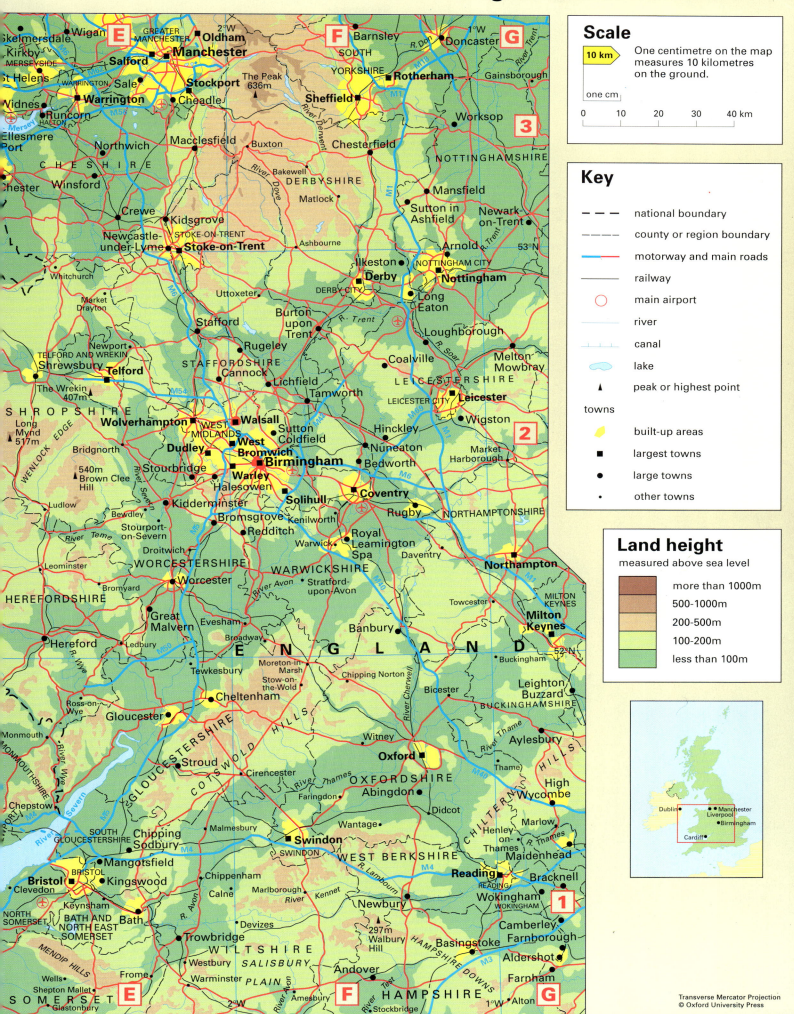

Transverse Mercator Projection
© Oxford University Press

Scale

10 km ▷ One centimetre on the map measures 10 kilometres on the ground.

one cm

0   10   20   30   40 km

Transverse Mercator Projection
© Oxford University Press

Key

- ▬▪▬▪ international boundary
- ▬ ▬ national boundary
- ▬ ─ county or region boundary
- ▬▬ motorway and main roads
- ─── railway
- ✈ main airport
- ~~~ river
- ┼┼┼ canal
- ⬭ lake
- ▲ peak or highest point

towns

- ▮ built-up areas
- ■ largest towns
- ● large towns
- • other towns

Land height

measured above sea level

- more than 1000m
- 500-1000m
- 200-500m
- 100-200m
- less than 100m
- below sea level

Transverse Mercator Projection
© Oxford University Press

28 South West England

Scale

10 km

One centimetre on the map measures 10 kilometres on the ground.

one cm

| 0 | 10 | 20 | 30 | 40 km |

Key

- ·–·–·– international boundary
- – – – national boundary
- – – – – county or region boundary
- —— motorway and main roads
- —— railway
- ⊕ main airport
- —— river
- ⊔⊔⊔ canal
- lake
- ▲ peak or highest point

towns

- built-up areas
- ■ largest towns
- ● large towns
- · other towns

Land height
measured above sea level

- more than 1000m
- 500-1000m
- 200-500m
- 100-200m
- less than 100m

Transverse Mercator Projection
© Oxford University Press

Most people in the United Kingdom live in large towns or cities.

Total number of people, 1991

England	48 million
Scotland	5 million
Wales	3 million
N. Ireland	2 million
U.K.	**58 million**

one kilometre · one kilometre

More than 250 people live in this square kilometre.

one kilometre · one kilometre

About 100 people live in this square kilometre.

one kilometre · one kilometre

Fewer than 50 people live in this square kilometre.

Transverse Mercator Projection
© Oxford University Press

Scale

45 km   One centimetre on the map measures 45 kilometres on the ground.

one cm

0	45	90	135	180 km

Key

■ cities with more than a million people

very many people

many people

few people

national boundary

international boundary

Manchester

Liverpool

Birmingham

London

The United Kingdom

Scale

45 km One centimetre on the map measures 45 kilometres on the ground.

one cm

0	45	90	135	180 km

Farmers produce food by growing crops and keeping animals.

Key

■	mostly livestock farms	cattle are kept for meat
■	mostly hill farms	sheep are kept for meat and wool
■	mostly dairy farms	cows are kept for milk
■	mostly arable farms	crops are grown

Many farms in Britain are mixed farms. Farmers grow crops *and* keep animals.

🌲	forestry	trees are planted for wood
✳	market gardening	fruit and vegetables are grown
▥	no farming	built-up areas

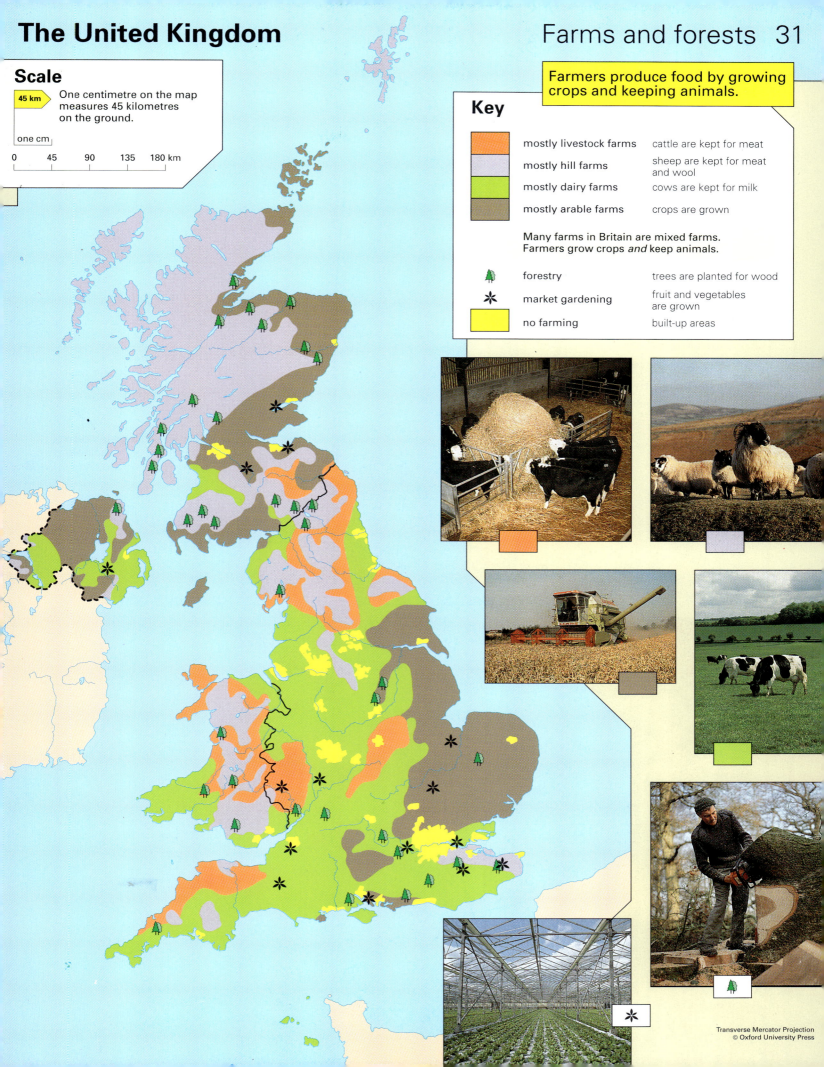

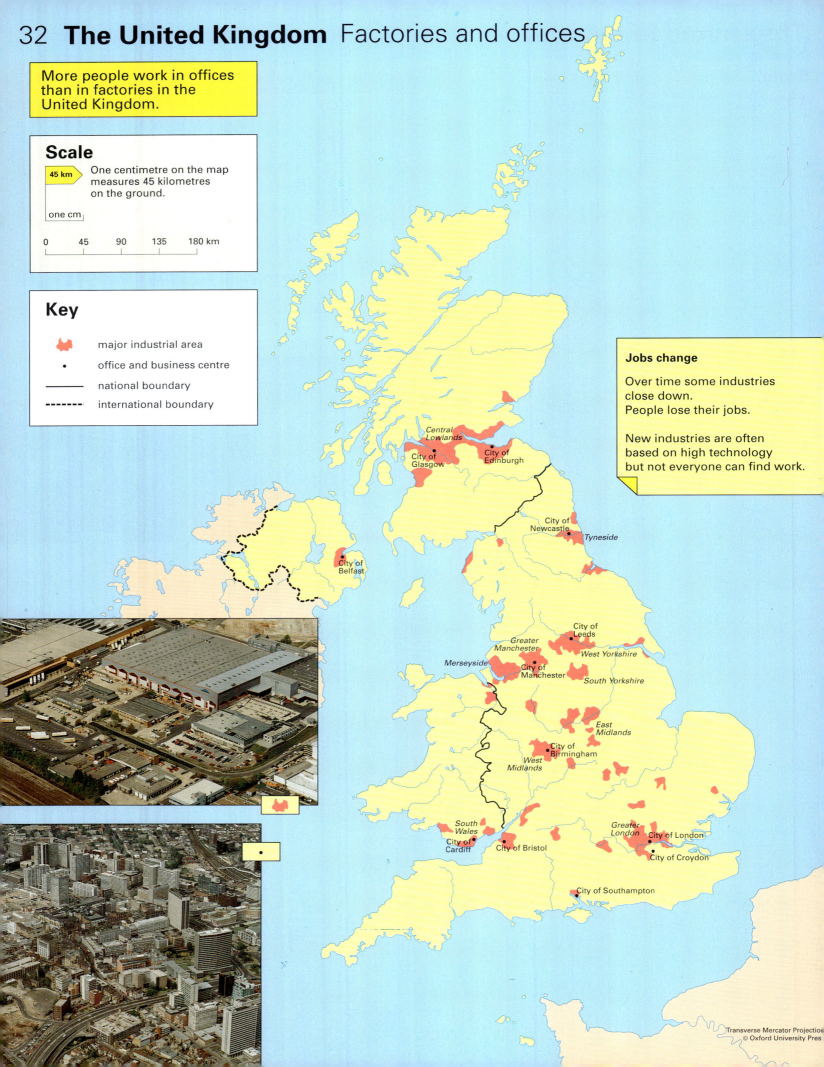

More people work in offices than in factories in the United Kingdom.

Scale

45 km   One centimetre on the map measures 45 kilometres on the ground.

one cm

0	45	90	135	180 km

Key

🔶   major industrial area

•   office and business centre

——   national boundary

------   international boundary

Jobs change

Over time some industries close down.
People lose their jobs.

New industries are often based on high technology but not everyone can find work.

Central Lowlands

City of Glasgow

City of Edinburgh

City of Newcastle

Tyneside

City of Belfast

Greater Manchester

City of Leeds

West Yorkshire

Merseyside

City of Manchester

South Yorkshire

East Midlands

City of Birmingham

West Midlands

South Wales

City of Cardiff

City of Bristol

Greater London

City of London

City of Croydon

City of Southampton

Transverse Mercator Projection
© Oxford University Press

Coal, oil, and natural gas hold energy which originally came from the sun.

Scale

60 km
One centimetre on the map measures 60 kilometres on the ground.

one cm

0   60   120   180   240 km

Key

- largest coal mines
- gas field and pipeline
- oil field and pipeline

largest power stations
- burning coal, oil or gas
- using water power
- using nuclear power
- using wind power

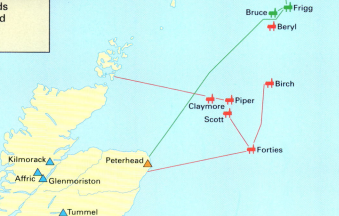
Oil and gas fields have drilling and pumping rigs

wind generator

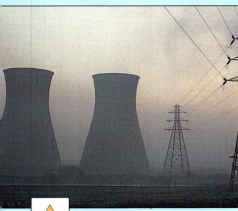
power station burning coal

Magnus
Tern
Statfjord
Brent
Ninian
North Alwyn
Foinaven
Bruce
Frigg
Beryl
Birch
Claymore
Piper
Scott
Forties
Fulmar
Peterhead

Kilmorack
Affric
Glenmoriston
Tummel
Cruachan
Breadalbane
Sloy
Longannet
Longannet
Torness
Hunterston
Cockenzie

Ellington
Blyth Harbour

Hartlepool
Teesside

Heysham
South Morecambe
Coal Clough
Riccall
Wistow
Whitemoor
Drax
Ravenspurn
West Sole
Ferrybridge
Eggborough
Pickerill
Harworth
West Burton
Cottam
Indefatigable
Thoresby
Hewett
Leman
Dinorwig
Fiddler's Ferry
Ratcliffe-on-Soar
Ashfordby
Mynydd Cemmaes
Penrhyddlan Llidiartywaun
Daw Mill
Sizewell
Ballylumford
Tower
Tilbury
Didcot
Grain
Aberthaw
Kingsnorth
Hinkley
Delabole
Carland Cross
Wytch Farm

Electricity is made in power stations

Thermal power stations burn coal, oil, or gas to make steam which drives turbines. Nuclear power stations use the heat from a nuclear reaction. Hydro electric power stations use water power. Wind power stations use wind generators.

Transverse Mercator Projection
© Oxford University Press

Roads and railways do not always take the shortest route between places.

Scale

45 km One centimetre on the map measures 45 kilometres on the ground.

one cm

0   45   90   135   180 km

Key

— major road
— motorway
— main railway
• road or rail terminal
built-up areas
land over 200 metres
land below 200 metres
— national boundary

valley of the River Taff near Cardiff, South Wales

Inverness
Aberdeen
Dundee
Glasgow
Edinburgh
M90
M9
M8
M74
M80
Coleraine
Londonderry
Larne
M2
Belfast
M1
Newry
Stranraer
Newcastle upon Tyne
Middlesbrough
A1(M)
M6
Kingston upon Hull
Leeds
M62
Liverpool
Manchester
M180
M1
Holyhead
M56
Sheffield
Nottingham
M1
Leicester
Norwich
M54
Birmingham
M5
M42
M6
A1(M)
M11
Fishguard
M50
M40
M1
M4
Cardiff
Bristol
M4
London
M25
M23
M20
M2
Dover
Folkestone
Channel Tunnel
Calais
M5
Southampton
M27
Weymouth
Penzance

bypass, Cannington, Somerset

Modern roads and motorways have gentle curves and often bypass towns to allow traffic to move at higher speeds. Rail networks avoid steep gradients.

F R A N C E

Transverse Mercator Projection
© Oxford University Press

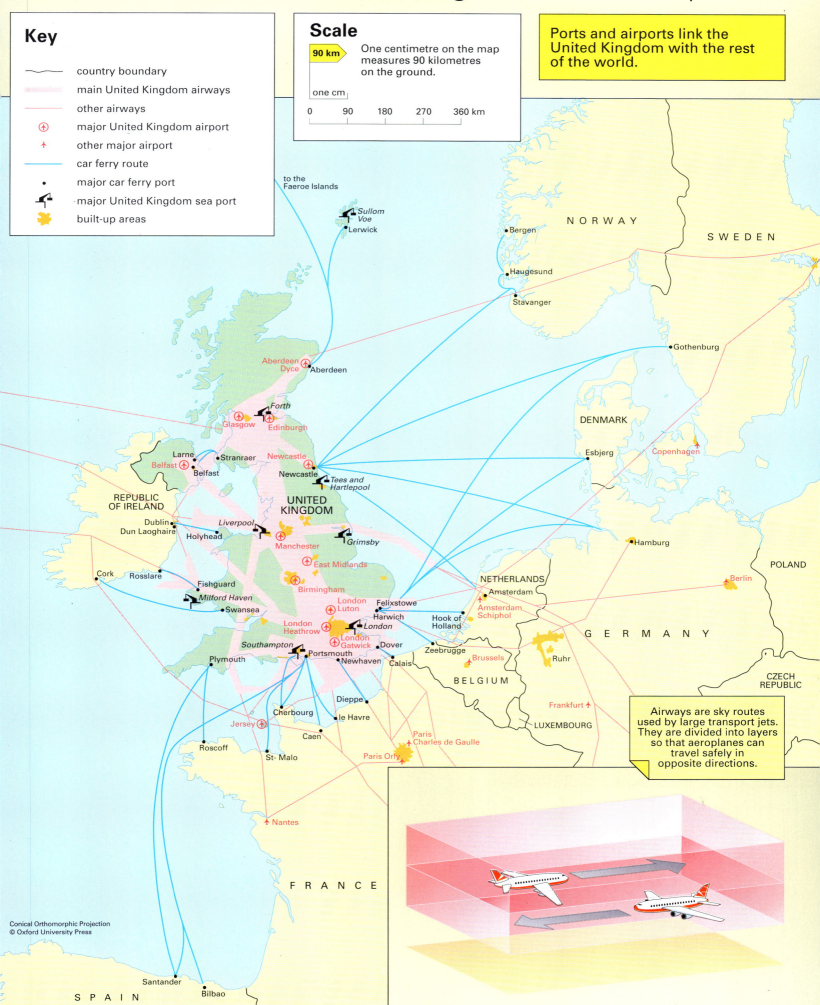

Key

- country boundary
- main United Kingdom airways
- other airways
- ⊕ major United Kingdom airport
- ✈ other major airport
- car ferry route
- • major car ferry port
- ⚓ major United Kingdom sea port
- built-up areas

Scale

90 km One centimetre on the map measures 90 kilometres on the ground.

one cm

0 90 180 270 360 km

Ports and airports link the United Kingdom with the rest of the world.

Airways are sky routes used by large transport jets. They are divided into layers so that aeroplanes can travel safely in opposite directions.

Conical Orthomorphic Projection
© Oxford University Press

NORWAY
SWEDEN
Bergen
Haugesund
Stavanger
Gothenburg
DENMARK
Esbjerg
Copenhagen
Hamburg
POLAND
Berlin
NETHERLANDS
Amsterdam
Amsterdam Schiphol
Hook of Holland
GERMANY
Ruhr
CZECH REPUBLIC
Zeebrugge
Brussels
BELGIUM
Frankfurt
LUXEMBOURG

to the Faeroe Islands
Sullom Voe
Lerwick

Aberdeen Dyce Aberdeen
Forth
Glasgow Edinburgh
Larne Stranraer
Belfast Belfast
Newcastle Newcastle
Tees and Hartlepool

REPUBLIC OF IRELAND
UNITED KINGDOM
Dublin
Dun Laoghaire
Liverpool
Holyhead
Manchester
Grimsby
East Midlands
Cork
Rosslare
Fishguard
Birmingham
Milford Haven
Swansea
Felixstowe
London Luton
Harwich
London Heathrow
London
London Gatwick
Dover
Calais
Southampton
Portsmouth
Newhaven
Plymouth
Dieppe
Cherbourg
le Havre
Jersey
Caen
Roscoff
St- Malo
Nantes
Paris Charles de Gaulle
Paris Orly

FRANCE
SPAIN
Santander
Bilbao

Damage to our land, sea, and air is called pollution.

Scale

45 km → One centimetre on the map measures 45 kilometres on the ground.

one cm

| 0 | 45 | 90 | 135 | 180 km |

Key

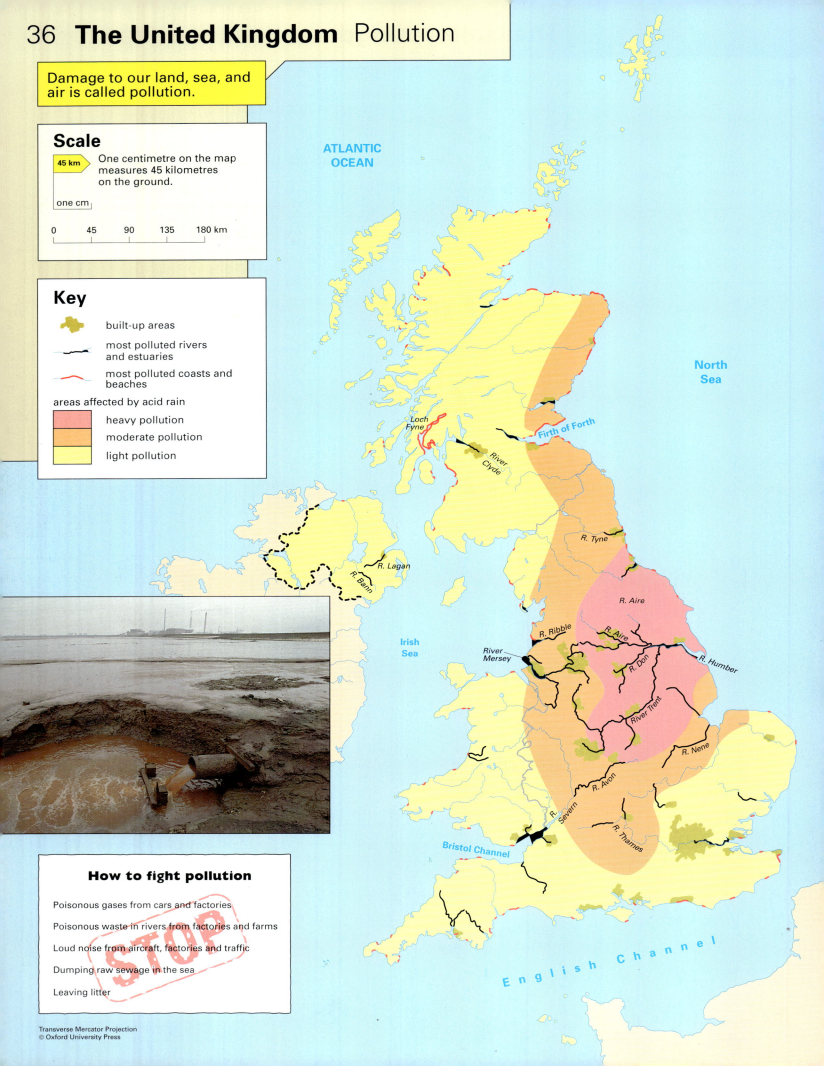

built-up areas

most polluted rivers and estuaries

most polluted coasts and beaches

areas affected by acid rain

heavy pollution

moderate pollution

light pollution

ATLANTIC OCEAN

North Sea

Loch Fyne

Firth of Forth

River Clyde

R. Lagan

R. Bann

R. Tyne

R. Aire

Irish Sea

R. Ribble

R. Aire

River Mersey

R. Don

R. Humber

River Trent

R. Nene

R. Avon

R. Severn

R. Thames

Bristol Channel

English Channel

How to fight pollution

Poisonous gases from cars and factories

Poisonous waste in rivers from factories and farms

Loud noise from aircraft, factories and traffic

Dumping raw sewage in the sea

Leaving litter

STOP

Transverse Mercator Projection
© Oxford University Press

Protecting nature, resources, and buildings is called conservation.

Scale

| 45 km | One centimetre on the map measures 45 kilometres on the ground. |

one cm

| 0 | 45 | 90 | 135 | 180 km |

Key

- National Parks
- areas of outstanding scenery and beauty
- protected coast
- ★ World Heritage Sites
- major built-up areas

National Park
Snowdonia

Area of outstanding scenery and beauty
Countryside in the Cotswolds

Protected coast
The Dorset coast at Durdle Door

★ **World Heritage Site**
Stonehenge

★ St Kilda

South Lewis, Harris and North Uist

Wester Ross

Cairngorm Mountains

Aberdeen

Ben Nevis and

Dundee

Jura

Loch Lomond

Edinburgh

Glasgow

Upper Tweeddale

Giant's Causeway

Antrim Coast and Glens

Sperrin

Belfast

Mourne

Northumberland

Hadrian's Wall

Newcastle upon Tyne

North Pennines

Durham Castle/ Cathedral

Middlesbrough

Lake District

Yorkshire Dales

North York Moors

Nidderdale

Forest of Bowland

Fountain's Abbey/ Studley Royal Park

Leeds

Kingston upon Hull

Liverpool

Manchester

Sheffield

Anglesey

Clwydian Range

Peak District

Lincolnshire Wolds

LLeyn

Snowdonia

Castles/Town Walls of King Edward

Ironbridge Gorge

Nottingham

Norfolk Coast

Shropshire Hills

Birmingham

Leicester

Norwich

The Broads Authority

Pembrokeshire Coast

Brecon Beacons

Wye Valley

Blenheim Palace

Suffolk Coast and Heaths

Cotswolds

Chilterns

London

Gower

Cardiff

Bristol

North Wessex Downs

Surrey Hills

Westminster Palace/ Abbey

Kent Downs

★ Bath

Stonehenge/ Avebury

High Weald

Exmoor

Cranbourne Chase

Southampton

Sussex Downs

Blackdown Hills

New Forest

Dartmoor

Dorset

Bodmin Moor

Isle of Wight

Transverse Mercator Projection
© Oxford University Press

Europe is the smallest continent but is the most crowded.

Key

Paris	cities with this type of lettering have more than 1 million people
■	capital cities
•	other cities
ITALY	the names of countries are shown in this type of lettering
∿	country boundary

Scale

300 km

One centimetre on the map measures 300 kilometres on the ground at the Equator.

one cm

0	300	600	900	1200 km

Population		692 000 000 people
Largest countries France (European part of Russia		547 026 sq km 3 955 400 sq km)
Countries with the most people Germany (European part of Russia		80 800 000 people 105 000 000 people)
Largest cities Paris (France) Moscow (Russia) London (UK)		9 319 000 people 8 801 000 people 6 378 000 people

Modified Gall Projection
© Oxford University Press

OCEAN

60°E

E **F**

3

Arctic Circle

60°N

FEDERATION (RUSSIA)

• Perm

• Nizhniy
Novgorod

• Kazan

• Ufa

2

• Samara

• Volgograd

onetsk

• Rostov-
on-Don

40°N

GEORGIA
Tbilisi ■

1

TURKEY

E

40°E

Modified Gall Projection
© Oxford University Press

The European Union

20°W

60°N

Arctic Circle

0°

Prime Meridian

40°N

60°N

20°W

0°

20°E

40°E

The European Union

The European Union is a group of countries which have agreed to work together and share the same plans for industry, agriculture, transport, and trade.

Key

~ country boundary

countries which are members of the European Union

countries which have applied to be members of the European Union

other European countries

Scale for both small maps

650 km

One centimetre on the map measures 650 kilometres on the ground at the Equator.

one cm

0   650   1300   1950   2600 km

How big is Europe?

20°W

Arctic Circle

0°

Prime Meridian

60°N

See how long journeys within Europe take, by air ✈ and by rail 🚄

3.5 hours ✈   Moscow

London

Berlin   🚄 **35.5 hours**

1 hour

Paris 🚄

3.4 hours ✈

15 hours

Rome

40°N

Athens

60°N

40°N

20°W

0°

20°E

40°E

Europe is a continent of peninsulas and islands.

A   20°W   B   Arctic Circle   0°   C

Iceland

1491m △
Mount
Hekla

3

N

*Faeroe
Islands*

*Shetland
Is'ands*

60°N

*Outer
Hebrides*

*Orkney
Islands*

Ben
Nevis
△1344m

North
Sea

Ireland

*Great
Britain*

R. Thames

English Channel

2

*Channel
Islands*

River Loire

R. Seine

ATLANTIC
OCEAN

Bay of
Biscay

*MASSIF
CENTRAL*

R. Rhône

River Rhine

4807m △
Mont
Blanc

A L P S

River Po

River Duero

River Ebro

PYRENEES

MESETA

40°N

River Tagus

Balearic Islands

Corsica

Minorca

Sardinia

Ibiza

Majorca

Tyrrhenian
Sea

A P P E N N I N E S

Adriatic Sea

1

A   20°W   B

Strait of
Gibraltar

Malta

Sicily

3323m △
Mount
Etna

Ionian
Sea

Peloponnese

Crete

M e d i t e r r a n e a n   S e a

*Lofoten
Islands*

North Cape   D   ARCTIC

S C A N D I N A V I A N   H I G H L A N D S

20°E

Kola
Peninsula

White
Sea

2469m △
Galdhøpiggen

R. Glomma

Lake
Vänern

Gulf of Bothnia

Lake
Oneg

Lake
Ladoga

Baltic Sea

Gotland

Bornholm

Lake
Peipus

River Elbe

Friesian Islands

River Vistula

N O R T H   E U R O P E A N   P L A I N

Pripet
Marshes

River Danube

C A R P A T H I A N S

River Dniester

River Dnieper

River Danube

2917m △
Mount Olympus

Sea of
Azov

Black Sea

A N A T O L I A N
PLATEAU

Aegean
Sea

TAURUS
MOUNTAINS

Cyprus

Prime Meridian

0°

C

20°E

D

Key

Colours show the height of the land.

	more than 2000 metres
	1000 – 2000 metres
	500 – 1000 metres
	200 – 500 metres
	less than 200 metres
	this land is below the level of the sea
▲	peak or highest point
	river
	lake
	marsh
	ice cap

Scale

300 km   One centimetre on the map measures 300 kilometres on the ground.

one cm

0   300   600   900   1200 km

	Area	10 498 000 sq km
	Highest peak Mount Elbrus Mont Blanc	5 642 m 4 807 m
	Lowest point Caspian Sea	28 m below sea level
	Largest freshwater lake Ladoga	18 390 sq km
	Longest river Volga	3 688 km

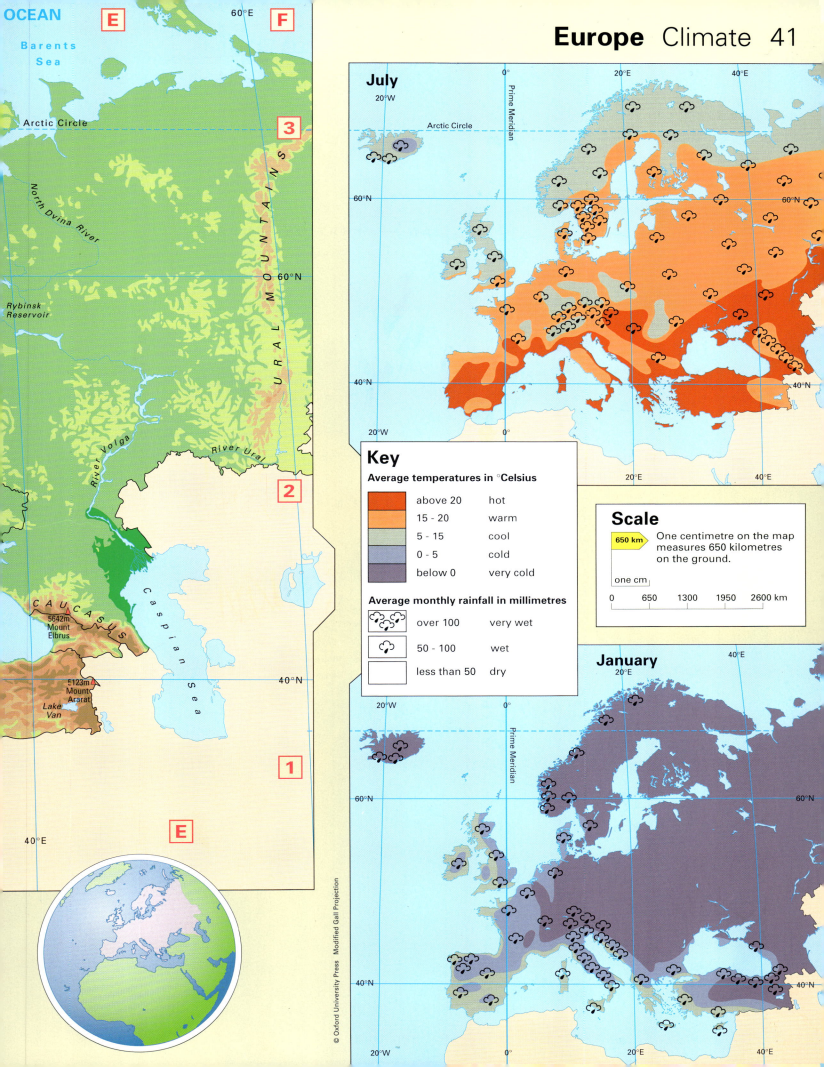

Of all the continents, Asia has the greatest variety of landscapes and people.

Arctic Circle

RUSSIAN FEDERATION (RUSSIA)

• Yakutsk

60°N

• St Petersburg

• Perm

• Moscow

Nizhniy Novgorod

• Yekaterinburg

• Kazan

• Chelyabinsk

• Omsk

• Novosibirsk

• Ufa

• Samara

Akmola ■

KAZAKHSTAN

Ulan Bator •

MONGOLIA

• Harbin

• Volgograd

Gur'yev •

Changchun • • Jilin

Shenyang Fushun

• Rostov-on-Don

ARMENIA

• Baku

UZBEKISTAN

• Tashkent

Bishkek

KIRGYZSTAN

Jinzhou

Anshan

NORTH KOREA

Yerevan

AZERBAIJAN

Beijing • ■ Yingkou Dandong

40°N

TURKMENISTAN

■ Ashkhabad

Dushanbe ■

TAJIKISTAN

Taiyuan •

Tianjin

Dalian

Pyongyang

JAPAN

• Tabriz

Mashhad ■

Zibo

Seoul •

SOUTH KOREA

• Nagoya

Aleppo

Tehran ■

AFGHANISTAN

Jinan •

Qingdao

• Yokohama

SYRIA

Lanzhou •

Tokyo ■

Beirut

Damascus

Baghdad ■

Kabul ■

JAMMU AND KASHMIR

• Xi'an

Pusan

Kita-Kyushu

LEBANON

Amman

• Esfahan

Islamabad ■

Nanjing •

Osaka

ISRAEL

IRAQ

CHINA

Jerusalem

Basra

KUWAIT

IRAN

Lahore •

Chengdu •

Wuhan

• Shanghai

JORDAN

Kuwait City

Bus_hehr

PAKISTAN

Delhi ■

Chongqing •

Nanchang •

Hangzhou

Riyadh

BAHRAIN

QATAR

Kanpur •

Kathmandu •

NEPAL

■ BHUTAN

Thimpu

• Wenzhou

Doha • Abu Dhabi

• Jiddah

UNITED ARAB EMIRATES

• Muscat

Karachi ■

BANGLADESH

Dhaka ■

Guangzhou •

Taipei ■

Tropic of Cancer

SAUDI ARABIA

OMAN

Ahmadabad ■

Calcutta

Chittagong ■

Hanoi •

Hong Kong

TAIWAN

Kao-hsiung

YEMEN REPUBLIC

San'a ■

Mumbai (Bombay) •

INDIA

Hyderabad •

MYANMAR

Vientiane •

Rangoon •

LAOS

VIETNAM

THAILAND

• Manila

Quezon ■

PHILIPPINES

Bangalore •

Chennai (Madras) •

Bangkok ■

CAMBODIA

Phnom Penh •

• Ho Chi Minh City

SRI LANKA

Colombo ■

MALDIVES

MALAYSIA

BRUNEI DARUSSALAM

Bandar Seri Begawan ■

Medan •

Kuala Lumpur

SINGAPORE

Equator

Palembang •

Jakarta •

Semarang •

INDONESIA

Bandung •

Surabaya

20°S

INDIAN OCEAN

Tropic of Capricorn

Modified Gall Projection
© Oxford University Press

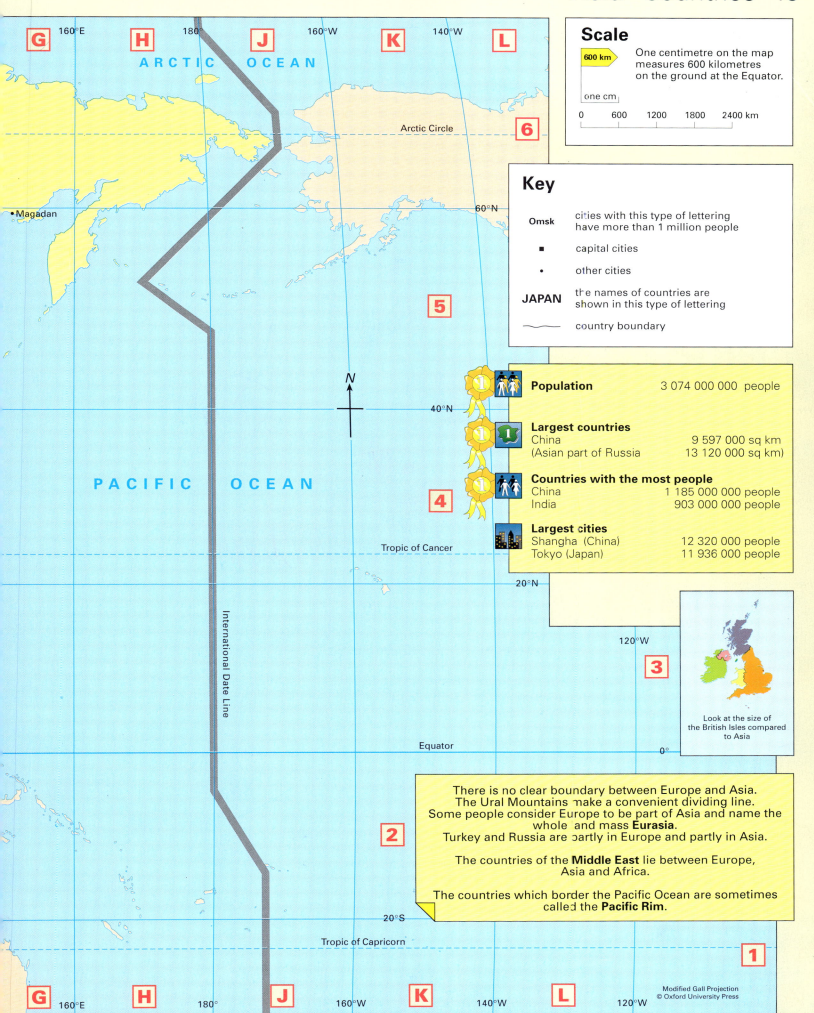

G 160°E H 180° J 160°W K 140°W L

ARCTIC OCEAN

Arctic Circle 6

• Magadan

60°N

5

PACIFIC OCEAN

N

40°N

International Date Line

4

Tropic of Cancer

20°N

120°W

3

Equator

2

20°S

Tropic of Capricorn

1

G 160°E H 180° J 160°W K 140°W L 120°W

Scale

600 km

One centimetre on the map measures 600 kilometres on the ground at the Equator.

one cm

0   600   1200   1800   2400 km

Key

Omsk — cities with this type of lettering have more than 1 million people

■ — capital cities

• — other cities

JAPAN — the names of countries are shown in this type of lettering

—— country boundary

Population 3 074 000 000 people

Largest countries
China 9 597 000 sq km
(Asian part of Russia 13 120 000 sq km)

Countries with the most people
China 1 185 000 000 people
India 903 000 000 people

Largest cities
Shangha (China) 12 320 000 people
Tokyo (Japan) 11 936 000 people

Look at the size of the British Isles compared to Asia

There is no clear boundary between Europe and Asia. The Ural Mountains make a convenient dividing line. Some people consider Europe to be part of Asia and name the whole land mass **Eurasia**. Turkey and Russia are partly in Europe and partly in Asia.

The countries of the **Middle East** lie between Europe, Asia and Africa.

The countries which border the Pacific Ocean are sometimes called the **Pacific Rim**.

Modified Gall Projection
© Oxford University Press

Asia covers one third of the land surface of the Earth.

ARCTIC OCEAN

G 160°E H 180° J 160°W K 140°W

6

River Kolyma

Arctic Circle

60°N

Bering Sea

Bering Strait

Kamchatka Peninsula

5

Kuril Islands

N

40°N

PACIFIC OCEAN

4

Tropic of Cancer

20°N

International Date Line

3

Equator 0°

20°S

Tropic of Capricorn

2

1

G 160°E H 180° J 160°W K 140°W

Scale

600 km

One centimetre on the map measures 600 kilometres on the ground at the Equator.

one cm

0   600   1200   1800   2400 km

Key

Colours show the height of the land.

more than 5000 metres
2000 – 5000 metres
1000 – 2000 metres
500 – 1000 metres
200 – 500 metres
less than 200 metres
this land is below the level of the sea

▲ peak or highest point

river

lake

marsh

desert

ice cap

Area   44 387 000 sq km

Highest peaks
Mount Everest   8 848 m
K2   8 611 m

Lowest point
Shores of the Dead Sea   395 m below sea level

Largest freshwater lake
Baykal   30 500 sq km

Longest river
Yangtze   6 380 km

Modified Gall Projection
© Oxford University Press

Many countries in Africa have no sea coast.

Key

Cairo — cities with this type of lettering have more than 1 million people

■ capital cities

• other cities

MALI — the names of countries are shown in this type of lettering

⎯ country boundary

Look at the size of the British Isles compared to Africa

ATLANTIC OCEAN

SOUTHERN OCEAN

INDIAN OCEAN

Tropic of Cancer

Equator

Tropic of Capricorn

Prime Meridian

Population — 613 566 000 people

Largest country — Sudan — 2 505 810 sq km

Country with the most people — Nigeria — 92 800 000 people

Largest cities
Cairo (Egypt) — 6 663 000 people
Kinshasa (Congo Dem. Rep.) — 3 804 000 people
Alexandria (Egypt) — 3 295 000 people

Scale — these maps of Africa are at the same scale

500 km — One centimetre on the map measures 500 kilometres on the ground at the Equator.

one cm

0   500   1000   1500   2000 km

Modified Gall Projection
© Oxford University Press

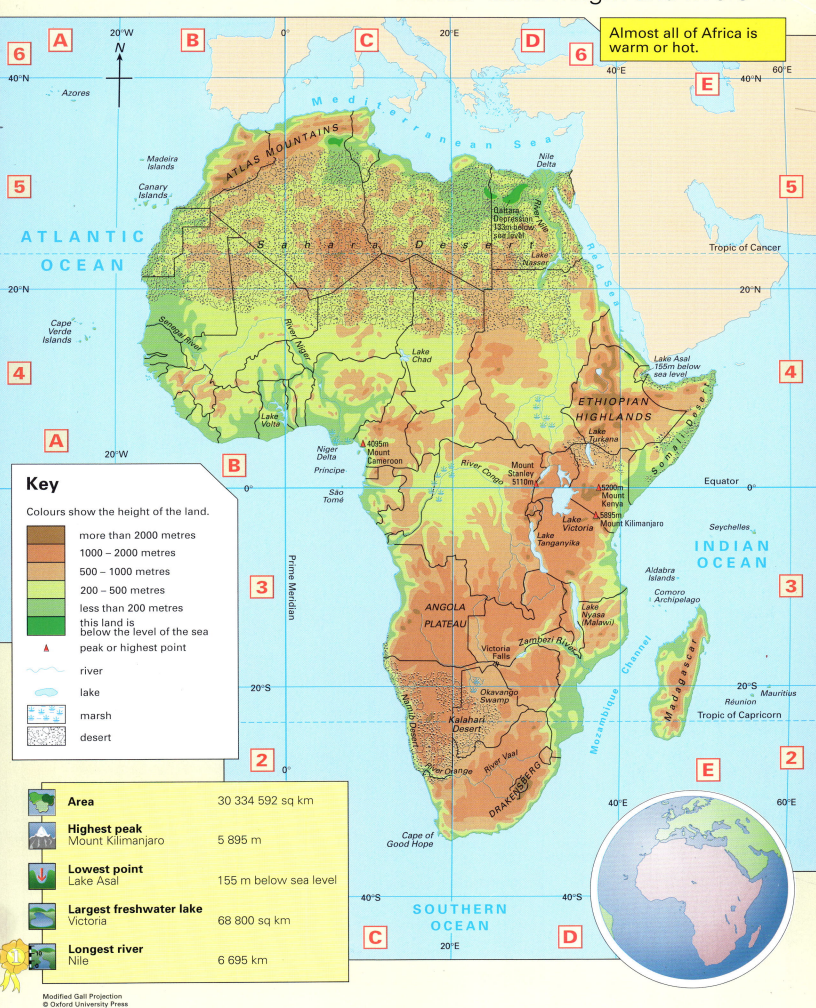

Almost all of Africa is warm or hot.

Key

Colours show the height of the land.

- more than 2000 metres
- 1000 – 2000 metres
- 500 – 1000 metres
- 200 – 500 metres
- less than 200 metres
- this land is below the level of the sea
- ▲ peak or highest point
- river
- lake
- marsh
- desert

Area	30 334 592 sq km	
Highest peak Mount Kilimanjaro	5 895 m	
Lowest point Lake Asal	155 m below sea level	
Largest freshwater lake Victoria	68 800 sq km	
Longest river Nile	6 695 km	

Modified Gall Projection
© Oxford University Press

Oceania is sometimes called Australasia.

20°N · C · 160°E · D · 180° · E · 20°N
160°W

A · 120°E · B · 140°E

4 · 4

MICRONESIA

Yap Islands

MARSHALL ISLANDS

P A C I F I C   O C E A N

0° · Equator · 0°

NAURU

K I R I B A T I

PAPUA NEW GUINEA

SOLOMON ISLANDS

TUVALU

SAMOA

3 · 3

Port Moresby

Honiara

VANUATU · • Vila

FIJI
Suva ■

INDIAN OCEAN

Darwin •

Wyndham •

Broome •

Cairns •

Townsville •

New Caledonia ■ Noumea

TONGA

20°S · 20°S
Tropic of Capricorn

Port Hedland

Tennant Creek

Mount Isa •

Alice • Springs

Longreach •

Rockhampton •

A U S T R A L I A

Geraldton •

Kalgoorlie •

Perth •

Lord Howe Island

Brisbane •

Cunnamulla •

Bourke •

Broken • Hill

Newcastle •

Sydney •

2 · 2

Esperance •

Port Augusta •

Albany •

Adelaide •

Canberra ■

Melbourne •

North Island

Auckland •

NEW ZEALAND

Hamilton •

New Plymouth •

Gisborne •

40°S · 40°S
160°W

Tasmania

• Launceston

Hobart •

Nelson • ■ Wellington

Greymouth •

Christchurch •

South Island

1 · 1

S O U T H E R N   O C E A N

Dunedin •

Invercargill •

A · 120°E · B · 140°E · C · 160°E · D

180°

E

Key

Sydney — cities with this type of lettering have more than 1 million people

■ — capital cities

• — other cities

FIJI — the names of countries are shown in this type of lettering

⌒ — country boundary

Population — 25 800 000 people

Largest country
Australia — 7 686 850 sq km

Country with the most people
Australia — 17 800 000 people

Largest cities
Sydney — 3 714 000 people
Melbourne — 3 189 000 people
(both these cities are in Australia)

Look at the size of the British Isles compared to Oceania

Scale

these maps of Oceania are at the same scale

500 km

One centimetre on the map measures 500 kilometres on the ground at the Equator.

one cm

0 · 500 · 1000 · 1500 · 2000 km

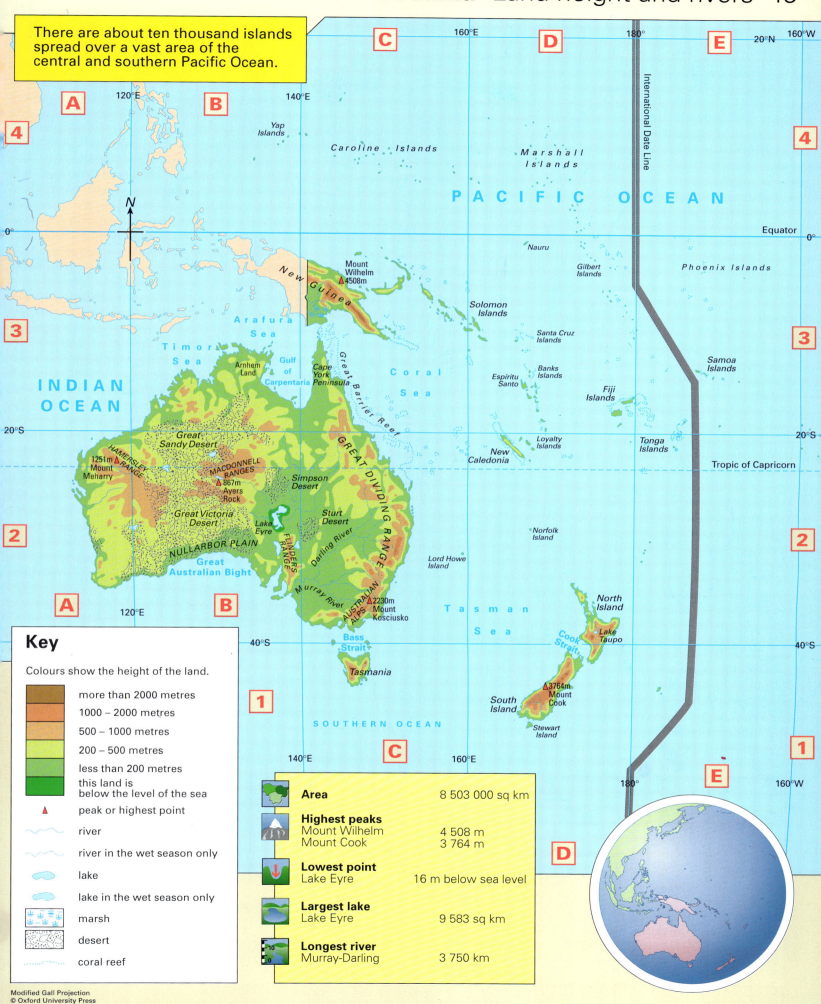

There are about ten thousand islands spread over a vast area of the central and southern Pacific Ocean.

PACIFIC OCEAN

160°E · 180° · 20°N · 160°W

120°E · 140°E

International Date Line

Yap Islands

Caroline Islands

Marshall Islands

0° Equator 0°

Nauru

Gilbert Islands

Phoenix Islands

Mount Wilhelm △4508m

New Guinea

Solomon Islands

Santa Cruz Islands

Samoa Islands

Arafura Sea

Timor Sea

Gulf of Carpentaria

Cape York Peninsula

Espíritu Santo

Banks Islands

Fiji Islands

Coral Sea

Great Barrier Reef

INDIAN OCEAN

Arnhem Land

20°S New Caledonia · Loyalty Islands · Tonga Islands · 20°S · Tropic of Capricorn

Great Sandy Desert

MACDONNELL RANGES

1251m △ Mount Meharry

HAMERSLEY RANGE

△ 867m Ayers Rock

Simpson Desert

GREAT DIVIDING RANGE

Great Victoria Desert

Lake Eyre

Sturt Desert

Darling River

Norfolk Island

NULLARBOR PLAIN

FLINDERS RANGE

Lord Howe Island

Great Australian Bight

Murray River

AUSTRALIAN ALPS

△2230m Mount Kosciusko

Tasman Sea

North Island

Lake Taupo

40°S · Bass Strait · Cook Strait · 40°S

Tasmania

South Island

△3764m Mount Cook

Stewart Island

SOUTHERN OCEAN

140°E · 160°E · 180° · 160°W

Key

Colours show the height of the land.

- more than 2000 metres
- 1000 – 2000 metres
- 500 – 1000 metres
- 200 – 500 metres
- less than 200 metres
- this land is below the level of the sea
- △ peak or highest point
- river
- river in the wet season only
- lake
- lake in the wet season only
- marsh
- desert
- coral reef

Area		8 503 000 sq km
Highest peaks Mount Wilhelm Mount Cook		4 508 m 3 764 m
Lowest point Lake Eyre		16 m below sea level
Largest lake Lake Eyre		9 583 sq km
Longest river Murray-Darling		3 750 km

Modified Gall Projection
© Oxford University Press

North America is dominated by the huge countries of the United States and Canada.

PACIFIC OCEAN

ATLANTIC OCEAN

Alaska

Arctic Circle

Inuvik

C A N A D A

Yellowknife

• Hay River

Anchorage

Prince Rupert

Edmonton

Calgary

Regina

Vancouver

Winnipeg

Seattle

Sudbury

Québec

St John's

Portland

Minneapolis

Ottawa

Montréal

Sydney

St Pierre and Miquelon

Milwaukee

Hamilton

Toronto

Buffalo

Boston

Halifax

Salt Lake City

Chicago

Detroit

Cleveland

Pittsburgh

Hartford

New York

Denver

Columbus

Indianapolis

Cincinnati

Philadelphia

San Francisco

Sacramento

Kansas City

St Louis

Baltimore

Washington D.C.

Las Vegas

UNITED STATES OF AMERICA

Norfolk

Los Angeles

Phoenix

Memphis

Charlotte

San Diego

Tucson

Dallas

Atlanta

El Paso

Jacksonville

Houston

San Antonio

New Orleans

Tampa

Monterrey

Miami

THE BAHAMAS

MEXICO

Nassau

Guadalajara

Havana

CUBA

DOMINICAN REPUBLIC

Santo Domingo

PUERTO RICO

México

Puebla

Port-au-Prince

San Juan

JAMAICA

HAITI

ANTIGUA AND BARBUDA

BELIZE

Kingston

ST KITTS-NEVIS

Belmopan

DOMINICA

GUATEMALA

HONDURAS

ST LUCIA

Guatemala

Tegucigalpa

ST VINCENT AND THE GRENADINES

BARBADOS

San Salvador

NICARAGUA

EL SALVADOR

Managua

GRENADA

San José

Panamá

TRINIDAD AND TOBAGO

COSTA RICA

PANAMA

Equator

Hawaiian Islands

Tropic of Cancer

Scale

these maps of North America are at the same scale

600 km

One centimetre on the map measures 600 kilometres on the ground at the Equator.

one cm

0	600	1200	1800	2400 km

Key

Miami — cities with this type of lettering have more than 1 million people

■ capital cities

• other cities

CUBA — the names of countries are shown in this type of lettering

~~ country boundary

Population — 415 778 000 people

Largest countries
Canada — 9 976 140 sq km
United States of America (USA) — 9 372 610 sq km
(The world's longest border is between the United States and Canada.)

Country with the most people
United States of America — 257 000 000 people

Largest cities
Mexico (Mexico) — 15 048 000 people
New York City (USA) — 7 333 253 people

Look at the size of the British Isles compared to North America

Modified Gall Projection
© Oxford University Press

The huge Rocky Mountain range forms the backbone of North America.

ARCTIC OCEAN

A **B** **C** **D** **E** **F** **G**

180°

160°W

140°W

120°W

100°W

80°W

60°W

Beaufort Sea

Arctic Circle

Yukon River

Mount McKinley 6194m △

Mount Logan 6050m

Gulf of Alaska

Bering Strait

Victoria Island

Great Bear Lake

Mackenzie River

Great Slave Lake

Slave R.

Baffin Island

Baffin Bay

Davis Strait

60°N

Bering Sea

Aleutian Islands

R O C K Y

M O U N T A I N S

Peace River

North Saskatchewan River

South Saskatchewan River

Hudson Bay

Nelson R.

Labrador

Newfoundland

N

Fraser R.

Vancouver Island

G R E A T

P L A I N S

Missouri River

Lake Winnipeg

Lake Superior

The Great Lakes

St. Lawrence River

40°N

Snake R.

SIERRA NEVADA

4418m △ Mount Whitney

Colorado R.

Death Valley 86m below sea level

Arkansas River

Mississippi River

Lake Huron

Lake Michigan

Lake Ontario

Lake Erie

Niagara Falls

APPALACHIAN MOUNTAINS

Bermuda

PACIFIC OCEAN

Gulf of California

Rio Grande

SIERRA MADRE

Tropic of Cancer

Hawaiian Islands

20°N

5452m △ △
Popocatépetl   5699m
Citlaltépetl

Yucatan Peninsula

Gulf of Mexico

Greater Antilles

W e s t   I n d i e s

Lesser Antilles

ATLANTIC OCEAN

Caribbean Sea

A **B** **C** **D** **E** **F** **G**

160°W

140°W

120°W

100°W

80°W

60°W

0°

Equator

Modified Gall Projection
© Oxford University Press

Key

Colours show the height of the land.

- more than 2000 metres
- 1000 – 2000 metres
- 500 – 1000 metres
- 200 – 500 metres
- less than 200 metres
- this land is below the level of the sea
- △ peak or highest point
- river
- lake
- marsh
- desert
- ice cap

Area		24 241 000 sq km
Highest peak Mount McKinley		6 194 m
Lowest point Death Valley		86 m below sea level
Largest freshwater lake Lake Superior		83 270 sq km
Longest river Mississippi-Missouri		6019 km

Brazilians speak Portuguese. Most other South Americans speak Spanish.

ATLANTIC OCEAN

N

Tropic of Cancer

20°N

PACIFIC OCEAN

Santa Marta
Barranquilla
Cartagena
Aruba *Netherlands Antilles*
Maracaibo **Caracas**
Valencia Barcelona
VENEZUELA Ciudad Guayana
Medellín Ciudad Bolívar Georgetown
Buenaventura **Bogotá** Paramaribo
Cali **GUYANA** Cayenne
COLOMBIA **SURINAME** **FRENCH GUIANA**
Boa Vista Ôiapoque
Quito Macapá

0° Equator

Galapagos Islands
ECUADOR
Guayaquil
Iquitos
Manaus Belém São Luís
Santarém **Fortaleza**
Teresina Natal
Pucallpa João Pessoa
PERU **Recife**
Lima Pôrto Velho **B R A Z I L** Aracaju
Cuzco **Salvador**
BOLIVIA
Arequipa Santa Cruz Cuiabá
La Paz **Brasília**
Arica Sucre Goiânia
Uberaba **Belo Horizonte**

20°S

Tropic of Capricorn
Antofagasta **PARAGUAY** Vitória
Salta Asunción Nova Iguaçu
C H I L E **São Paulo** **Rio de Janeiro**
Curitiba

ATLANTIC OCEAN

Córdoba **Pôrto Alegre**
Valparaíso Mendoza **URUGUAY**
Santiago **Rosario**
Concepción **Buenos Aires** **Montevideo**
ARGENTINA
Bahía Blanca Mar del Plata

40°S

Puerto Montt

Comodoro Rivadavia

Juan Fernandez Islands

Stanley
Falkland Islands

Punta Arenas

South Georgia

60°S

Scale

these maps of South America are at the same scale

500 km

One centimetre on the map measures 500 kilometres on the ground at the Equator.

one cm

| 0 | 500 | 1000 | 1500 | 2000 km |

Key

Lima   cities with this type of lettering have more than 1 million people

■   capital cities

•   other cities

PERU   the names of countries are shown in this type of lettering

‒‒‒   country boundary

Look at the size of the British Isles compared to South America

Population 283 519 000 people

Largest countries
Brazil 8 511 966 sq km
Argentina 2 776 890 sq km

Country with most people
Brazil 159 100 000 people

Largest cities
Buenos Aires (Argentina) 11 256 000 people
São Paulo (Brazil) 9 627 000 people
Rio de Janeiro (Brazil) 5 473 000 people

The Amazon rainforest contains half of all known plants and animals in the world.

Key

Colours show the height of the land.

- more than 5000 metres
- 2000 – 5000 metres
- 1000 – 2000 metres
- 500 – 1000 metres
- 200 – 500 metres
- less than 200 metres
- this land is below the level of the sea
- ▲ peak or highest point
- river
- lake
- marsh
- desert
- ice cap

Area	17 832 000 sq km	
Highest peaks		
Mount Aconcagua	6 960 m	
Ojos del Salado	6 908 m	
Lowest point		
Valdés Peninsula	40 m below sea level	
Largest freshwater lake		
Titicaca	8 340 sq km	
Longest river		
Amazon	6 516 km	
World's highest waterfall		
Angel Falls (Venezuela)	979 m	

Modified Gall Projection
© Oxford University Press

Antarctica has 90% of all of the ice in the world.

Scale

340 km

One centimetre on the map measures 340 kilometres on the ground.

one cm

| 0 | 340 | 680 | 1020 | 1360 km |

Area 13 340 000 sq km

Highest point
Vinson Massif 5 140 m

World's longest glacier
Lambert Glacier 400 km

Look at the size of the British Isles compared to Antarctica

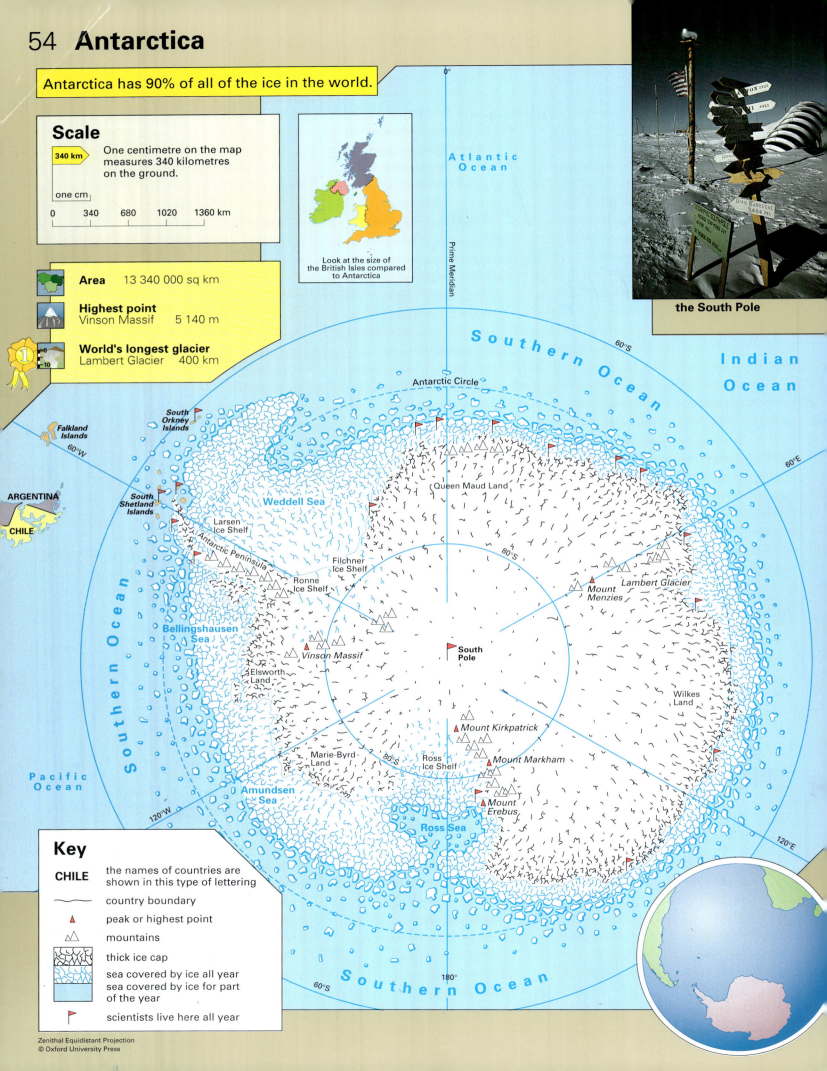

the South Pole

Atlantic Ocean

0°

Prime Meridian

Southern Ocean

60°S

Indian Ocean

Antarctic Circle

South Orkney Islands

Falkland Islands

60°W

ARGENTINA

CHILE

South Shetland Islands

Weddell Sea

Queen Maud Land

60°E

Larsen Ice Shelf

Antarctic Peninsula

Filchner Ice Shelf

80°S

Ronne Ice Shelf

Lambert Glacier

Mount Menzies

Southern Ocean

Bellingshausen Sea

Vinson Massif

South Pole

Wilkes Land

Elsworth Land

Pacific Ocean

80°S

Marie-Byrd Land

Mount Kirkpatrick

Ross Ice Shelf

Mount Markham

120°W

Amundsen Sea

Mount Erebus

120°E

Ross Sea

60°S

Southern Ocean

180°

Key

CHILE — the names of countries are shown in this type of lettering

— country boundary

▲ peak or highest point

△ mountains

▨ thick ice cap

▨ sea covered by ice all year

☐ sea covered by ice for part of the year

⚑ scientists live here all year

Most of the Arctic is a huge frozen ocean.

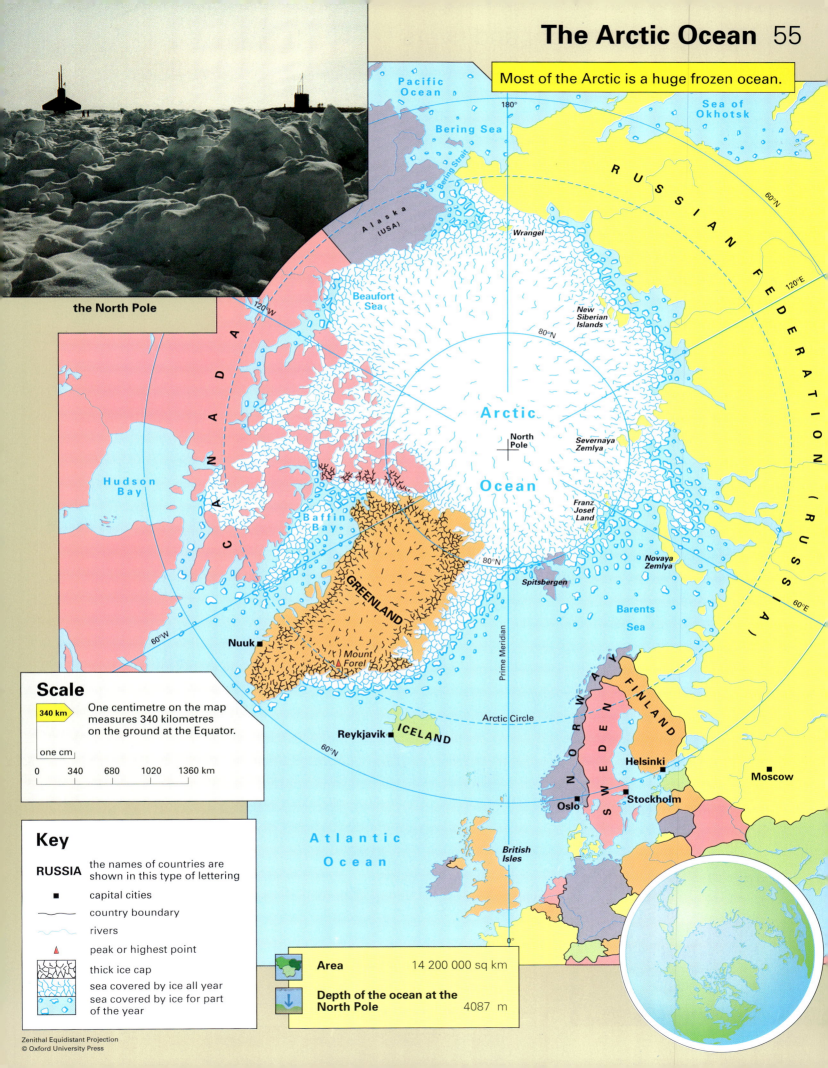

the North Pole

Pacific Ocean

Bering Sea

Sea of Okhotsk

Wrangel

R U S S I A N   F E D E R A T I O N   (R U S S I A)

60°N

180°

120°E

Alaska (USA)

Bering Strait

Beaufort Sea

New Siberian Islands

80°N

60°E

120°W

C A N A D A

Arctic

North Pole

Severnaya Zemlya

Ocean

Franz Josef Land

Hudson Bay

Baffin Bay

80°N

Novaya Zemlya

Spitsbergen

GREENLAND

Nuuk ■

▲ Mount Forel

Barents Sea

Prime Meridian

N O R W A Y

F I N L A N D

Arctic Circle

Reykjavik ■ **ICELAND**

60°N

S W E D E N

Helsinki ■

Moscow ■

A t l a n t i c   O c e a n

British Isles

Oslo ■ ■ Stockholm

0°

Scale

340 km

One centimetre on the map measures 340 kilometres on the ground at the Equator.

one cm

| 0 | 340 | 680 | 1020 | 1360 km |

Key

RUSSIA the names of countries are shown in this type of lettering

■ capital cities

country boundary

rivers

▲ peak or highest point

thick ice cap

sea covered by ice all year

sea covered by ice for part of the year

| **Area** | 14 200 000 sq km |
| **Depth of the ocean at the North Pole** | 4087 m |

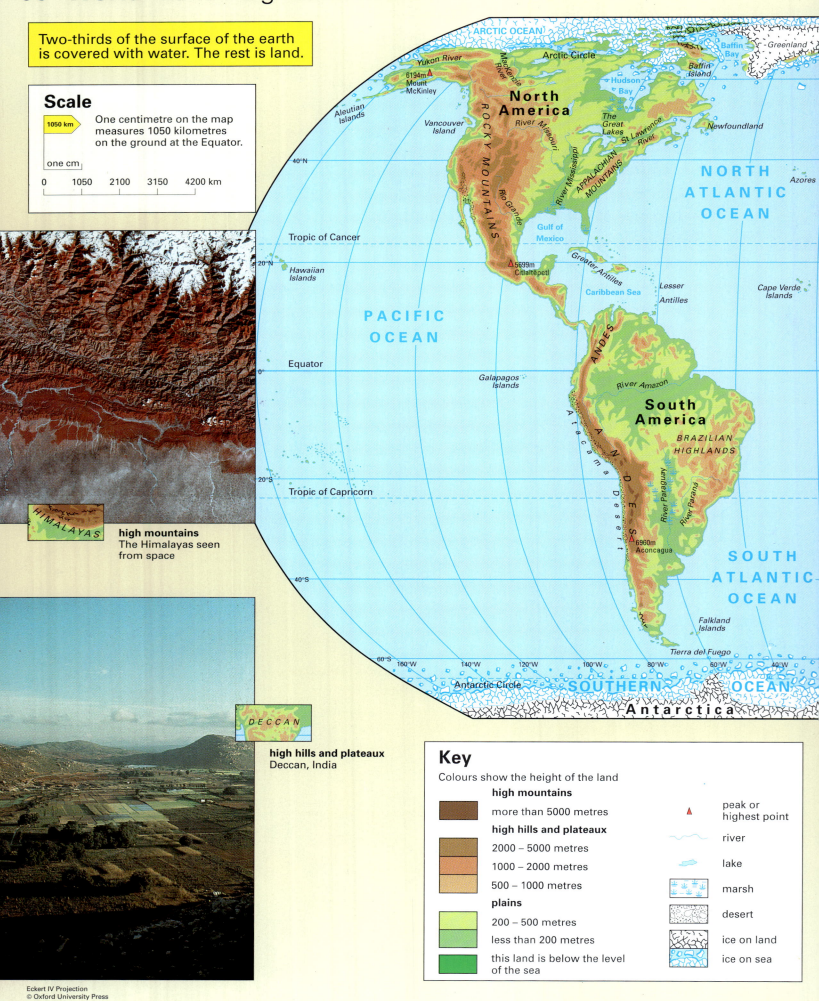

Two-thirds of the surface of the earth is covered with water. The rest is land.

Scale

1050 km

One centimetre on the map measures 1050 kilometres on the ground at the Equator.

one cm

| 0 | 1050 | 2100 | 3150 | 4200 km |

high mountains
The Himalayas seen from space

HIMALAYAS

DECCAN

high hills and plateaux
Deccan, India

ARCTIC OCEAN

Arctic Circle

Yukon River

Mackenzie River

6194m
Mount McKinley

North America

Greenland

Baffin Bay

Baffin Island

Hudson Bay

The Great Lakes

River Missouri

St Lawrence River

Newfoundland

Aleutian Islands

Vancouver Island

R O C K Y   M O U N T A I N S

Rio Grande

River Mississippi

APPALACHIAN MOUNTAINS

Gulf of Mexico

NORTH ATLANTIC OCEAN

Azores

40°N

Tropic of Cancer

20°N

Hawaiian Islands

5699m
Citlaltépetl

Greater Antilles

Caribbean Sea

Lesser Antilles

Cape Verde Islands

PACIFIC OCEAN

Equator

0°

Galapagos Islands

ANDES

River Amazon

South America

BRAZILIAN HIGHLANDS

20°S

Tropic of Capricorn

Atacama Desert

A N D E S

River Paraguay

River Parana

40°S

6960m
Aconcagua

SOUTH ATLANTIC OCEAN

Falkland Islands

Tierra del Fuego

60°S

160°W   140°W   120°W   100°W   80°W   60°W   40°W

Antarctic Circle

SOUTHERN   OCEAN

A n t a r c t i c a

Key

Colours show the height of the land

high mountains

more than 5000 metres

high hills and plateaux

2000 – 5000 metres

1000 – 2000 metres

500 – 1000 metres

plains

200 – 500 metres

less than 200 metres

this land is below the level of the sea

△ peak or highest point

river

lake

marsh

desert

ice on land

ice on sea

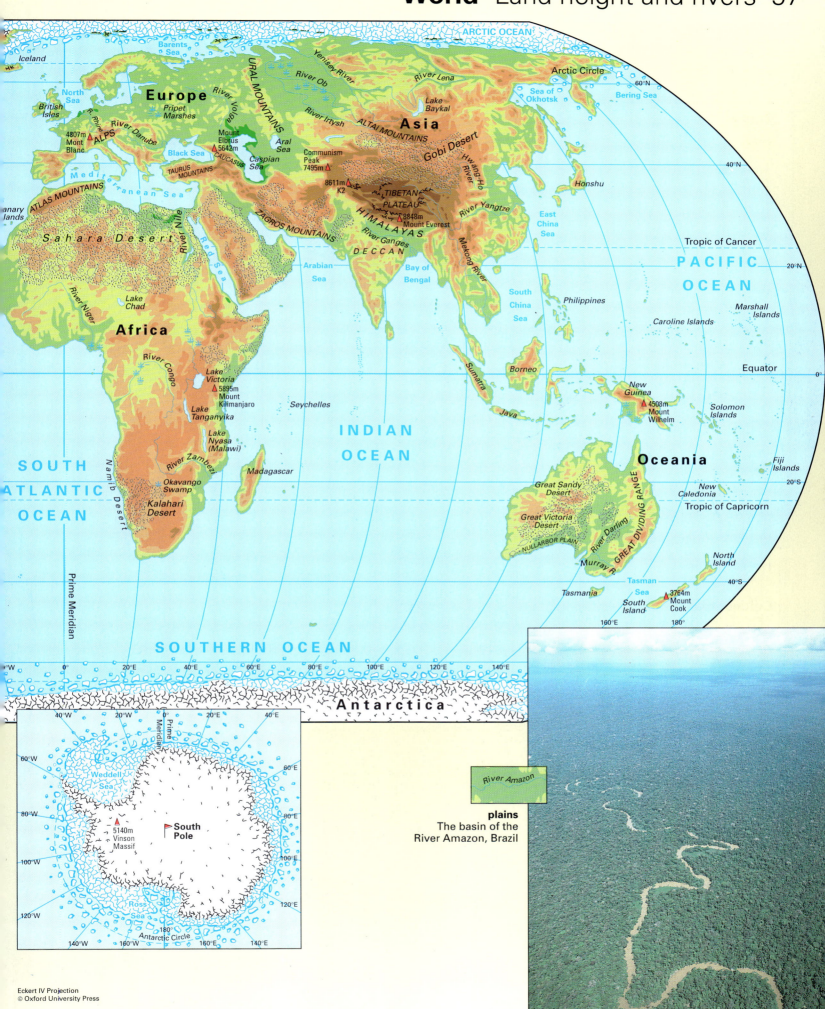

ARCTIC OCEAN

Iceland

Barents
Sea

North
Sea

*British
Isles*

Europe

*Pripet
Marshes*

R. Rhine
4807m
Mont
Blanc **ALPS**

River Danube

River Volga

URAL MOUNTAINS

River Ob

Yenisey River

River Lena

Arctic Circle

60°N

Sea of
Okhotsk

Bering Sea

Mount
Elbrus
5642m

Aral
Sea

River Irtysh

ALTAI MOUNTAINS

Asia

Lake
Baykal

40°N

Honshu

Black Sea

CAUCASUS

TAURUS
MOUNTAINS

Caspian
Sea

Communism
Peak
7495m

Gobi Desert

Hwang-Ho
River

Mediterranean Sea

8611m
K2

TIBETAN
PLATEAU

River Yangtze

East
China
Sea

ATLAS MOUNTAINS

*Canary
Islands*

River Nile

Red Sea

ZAGROS MOUNTAINS

HIMALAYAS

8848m
Mount Everest

Tropic of Cancer

Sahara Desert

*Arabian
Sea*

River Ganges

D E C C A N

Mekong River

PACIFIC

20°N

OCEAN

Bay of
Bengal

South
China
Sea

Philippines

*Marshall
Islands*

River Niger

Lake
Chad

Caroline Islands

Equator

Africa

River Congo

Lake
Victoria

5895m
Mount
Kilimanjaro

Seychelles

Sumatra

Borneo

*New
Guinea*

4508m
Mount
Wilhelm

*Solomon
Islands*

INDIAN

Java

OCEAN

Lake
Tanganyika

Lake
Nyasa
(Malawi)

SOUTH

River Zambezi

Madagascar

Oceania

*Fiji
Islands*

ATLANTIC

Namib Desert

Okavango
Swamp

20°S

OCEAN

*Kalahari
Desert*

*Great Sandy
Desert*

GREAT DIVIDING RANGE

*New
Caledonia*

Tropic of Capricorn

*Great Victoria
Desert*

River Darling

NULLARBOR PLAIN

*North
Island*

Prime Meridian

Murray R.

Tasman
Sea

40°S

SOUTHERN OCEAN

Tasmania

*South
Island*

3764m
Mount
Cook

160°E

180°

°W

0°

20°E

40°E

60°E

80°E

100°E

120°E

140°E

Antarctica

40°W

20°W

Prime Meridian

20°E

40°E

60°W

60°E

Weddell
Sea

80°W

80°E

5140m
Vinson
Massif

**South
Pole**

100°W

100°E

Ross
Sea

120°E

120°W

180°

140°W

160°W

160°E

140°E

Antarctic Circle

plains
The basin of the
River Amazon, Brazil

River Amazon

Eckert IV Projection
© Oxford University Press

Patterns of temperature and rainfall throughout the year make types of climate.

Scale

1050 km

One centimetre on the map measures 1050 kilometres on the ground at the Equator.

one cm

| 0 | 1050 | 2100 | 3150 | 4200 km |

Key

polar climate

continental climate

coastal climate

Mediterranean climate

desert climate

tropical climate

equatorial climate

high mountain climate

* places with record breaking climates

 Hottest place
Al' Aziziyah (Libya)

 Coldest place
Vostok (Antarctica)

 Driest place
Arica, Atacama Desert (Chile)

Wettest place
Mount Waialeale (Hawaii)

 Windiest place
Mount Washington (USA)

 Snowiest place
Mount Ranier (USA)

Mount Rainier *

Mount Washington *

Mount Waialeale

Arctic Circle

Tropic of Cancer

Equator

Tropic of Capricorn

Arica *

Antarctic Circle

Eckert IV Projection   © Oxford University Press

 polar climate
very cold all year

continental climate
very cold winters, warmer summers

coastal climate
warm summers, mild winters, rain all year

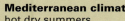 **Mediterranean climate**
hot dry summers, warm wet winters

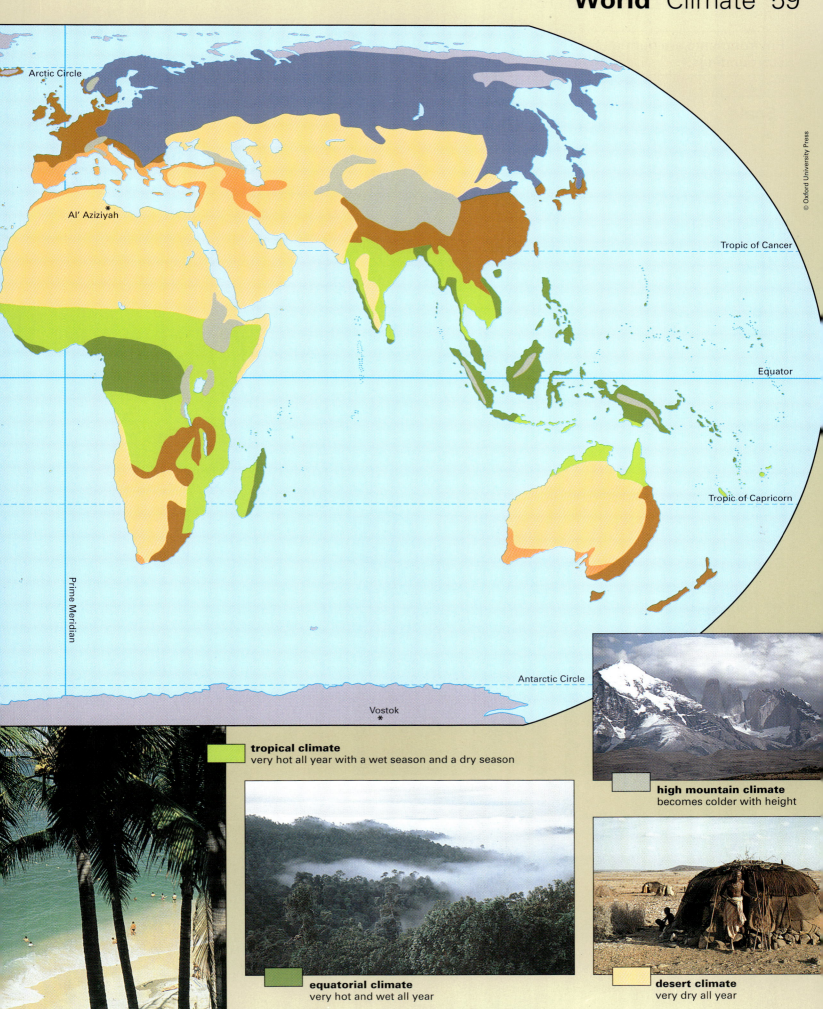

© Oxford University Press

Arctic Circle

Al' Aziziyah

Tropic of Cancer

Equator

Prime Meridian

Tropic of Capricorn

Antarctic Circle

Vostok

tropical climate
very hot all year with a wet season and a dry season

high mountain climate
becomes colder with height

equatorial climate
very hot and wet all year

desert climate
very dry all year

Environments are our natural surroundings.

Scale

One centimetre on the map measures 1050 kilometres on the ground at the Equator.

1050 km

one cm

| 0 | 1050 | 2100 | 3150 | 4200 km |

Key

△ high mountains

🌲 cold forest

savannah

🌳 hot forest

desert

marsh

ice on land

ice on the sea

very large built up areas

country boundary

Most environments have been influenced by people.

ARCTIC OCEAN

ROCKY MOUNTAINS

60°N

40°N

Chicago · New York · Philadelphia · San Francisco · Los Angeles

NORTH ATLANTIC OCEAN

Tropic of Cancer

20°N

Mexico

PACIFIC OCEAN

ANDES · Amazonia

Equator · 0°

Atacama Desert · ANDES

20°S · Tropic of Capricorn

Rio de Janeiro · São Paulo

SOUTH ATLANTIC OCEAN

40°S

Buenos Aires

160°W 140°W 120°W 100°W 80°W 40°W

very large built up area

desert

hot forest

cold forest

savannah

marsh

ARCTIC OCEAN

Arctic Circle

London
Paris
Ruhr
ALPS
Moscow
Istanbul
Cairo-Alexandria
Tehran
CAUCASUS
Siberia
Gobi Desert
Beijing
Seoul
Tokyo-Yokohama
Osaka-Kobe-Kyoto
Shanghai
Chungking
Sahara Desert
River Nile
Delhi
Karachi
Calcutta
Dhaka
HIMALAYAS
Mumbai
Manila

60°N
180
40°N
Tropic of Cancer
PACIFIC OCEAN
20°N

Equator

INDIAN OCEAN

Jakarta

SOUTH ATLANTIC OCEAN

Kalahari Desert

Great Victoria Desert

20°S
Tropic of Capricorn

40°S

Prime Meridian

SOUTHERN OCEAN

20°W   0°   20°E   40°E   60°E   80°E   100°E   120°E   140°E   60°S   160°E   180

Eckert IV Projection
© Oxford University Press

60°W
40°W   20°W   0°   20°E   40°E
Prime Meridian
80°W   60°E
South Pole
100°W   80°E
120°W   100°E
140°W   160°W   180   160°E   140°E   120°E
Antarctic Circle

ice

high mountains

People have damaged the environment in many parts of the world.

Scale

1050 km

One centimetre on the map measures 1050 kilometres on the ground at the Equator.

one cm

| 0 | 1050 | 2100 | 3150 | 4200 km |

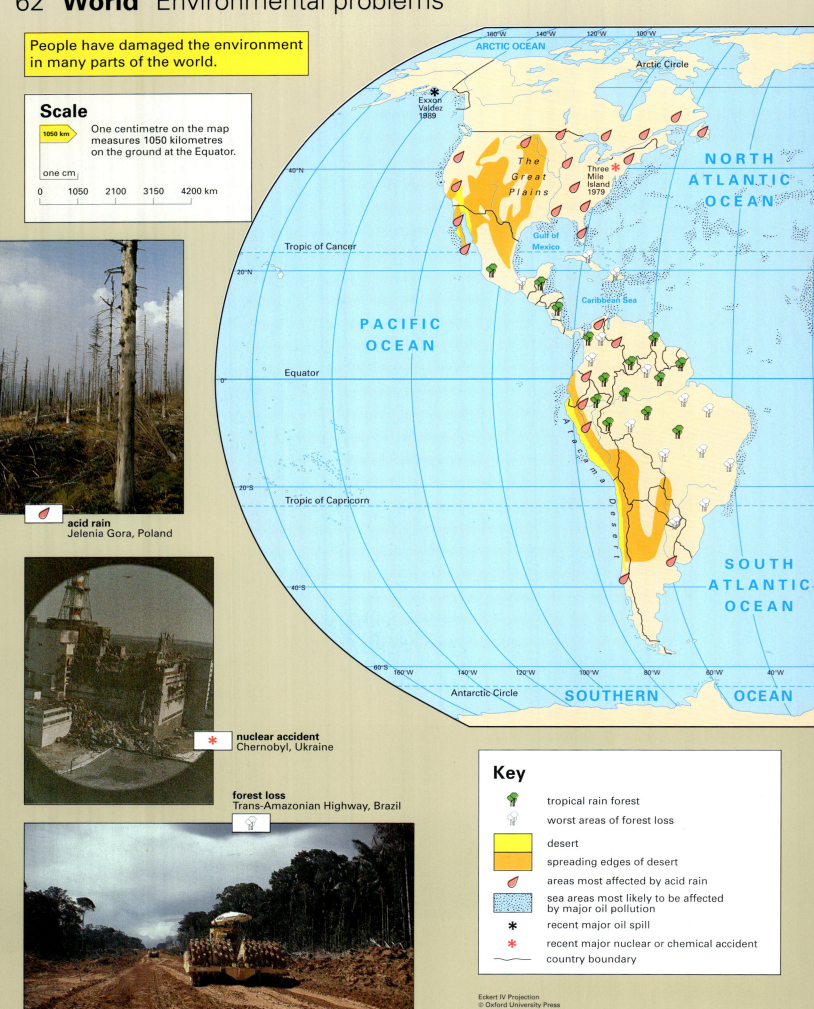

acid rain
Jelenia Gora, Poland

nuclear accident
Chernobyl, Ukraine

forest loss
Trans-Amazonian Highway, Brazil

ARCTIC OCEAN

Arctic Circle

Exxon Valdez 1989

NORTH ATLANTIC OCEAN

The Great Plains

Three Mile Island 1979

40°N

Tropic of Cancer

20°N

Gulf of Mexico

PACIFIC OCEAN

Caribbean Sea

Equator 0°

Atacama Desert

20°S

Tropic of Capricorn

SOUTH ATLANTIC OCEAN

40°S

60°S

Antarctic Circle

SOUTHERN OCEAN

Key

- tropical rain forest
- worst areas of forest loss
- desert
- spreading edges of desert
- areas most affected by acid rain
- sea areas most likely to be affected by major oil pollution
- recent major oil spill
- recent major nuclear or chemical accident
- country boundary

Eckert IV Projection
© Oxford University Press

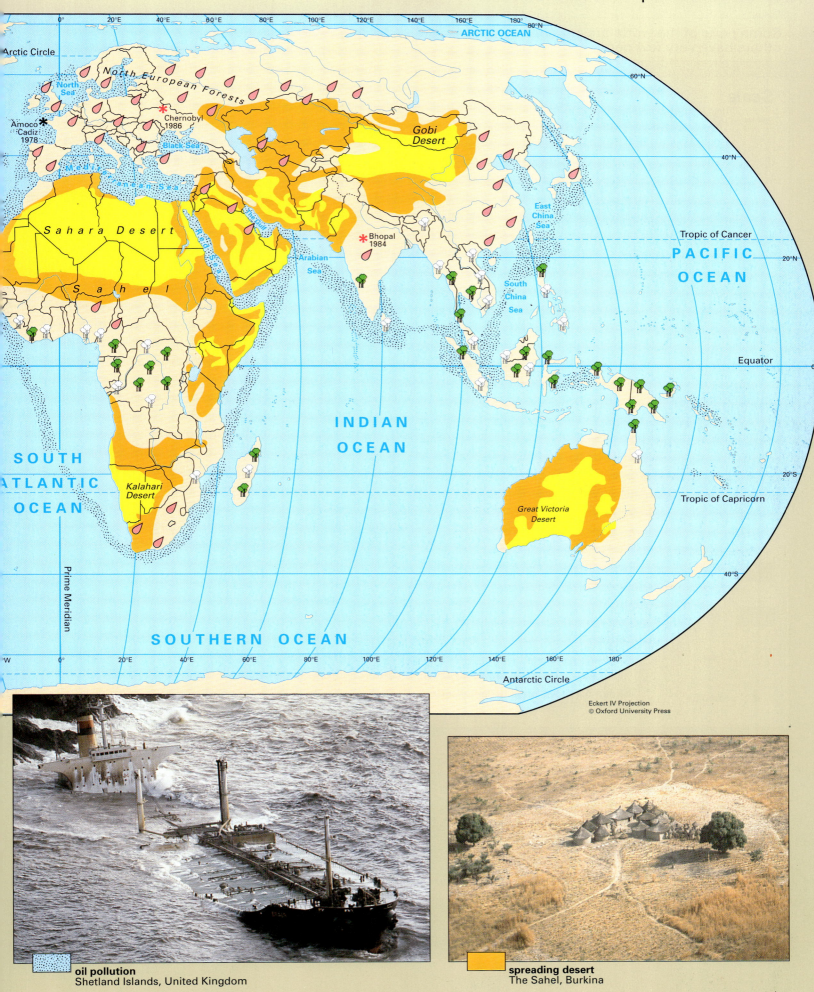

ARCTIC OCEAN

80°N

Arctic Circle

60°N

North European Forests

North
Sea

Amoco
Cadiz
1978

Chernobyl
1986

Black Sea

Mediterranean Sea

40°N

*Gobi
Desert*

East
China
Sea

Tropic of Cancer

**PACIFIC
OCEAN**

Sahara Desert

Bhopal
1984

20°N

Red Sea

Arabian
Sea

South
China
Sea

S a h e l

Equator

0°

**INDIAN
OCEAN**

**SOUTH
ATLANTIC
OCEAN**

*Kalahari
Desert*

20°S

*Great Victoria
Desert*

Tropic of Capricorn

Prime Meridian

40°S

SOUTHERN OCEAN

0°   20°E   40°E   60°E   80°E   100°E   120°E   140°E   160°E   180°

Antarctic Circle

Eckert IV Projection
© Oxford University Press

oil pollution
Shetland Islands, United Kingdom

spreading desert
The Sahel, Burkina

Some parts of the world are crowded, others have very few people.

Scale

1050 km

One centimetre on the map measures 1050 kilometres on the ground at the equator.

one cm

| 0 | 1050 | 2100 | 3150 | 4200 km |

Key

one million (1 000 000) people live near each dot

very many people

many people

few people

the world's largest cities. Each has more than 5 million people

Welfare

Some people in the world are rich. Many people are poor, or hungry, or suffering as a result of war.

rich countries — This colour shows the 25 richest countries in the world. Not everyone in these countries is rich but most live comfortably.

poor countries — This colour shows the 40 poorest countries in the world. Not everyone in these countries is poor but most are in need.

war — This symbol shows places where there has recently been a war.

famine — This symbol shows places where there has recently been a shortage of food.

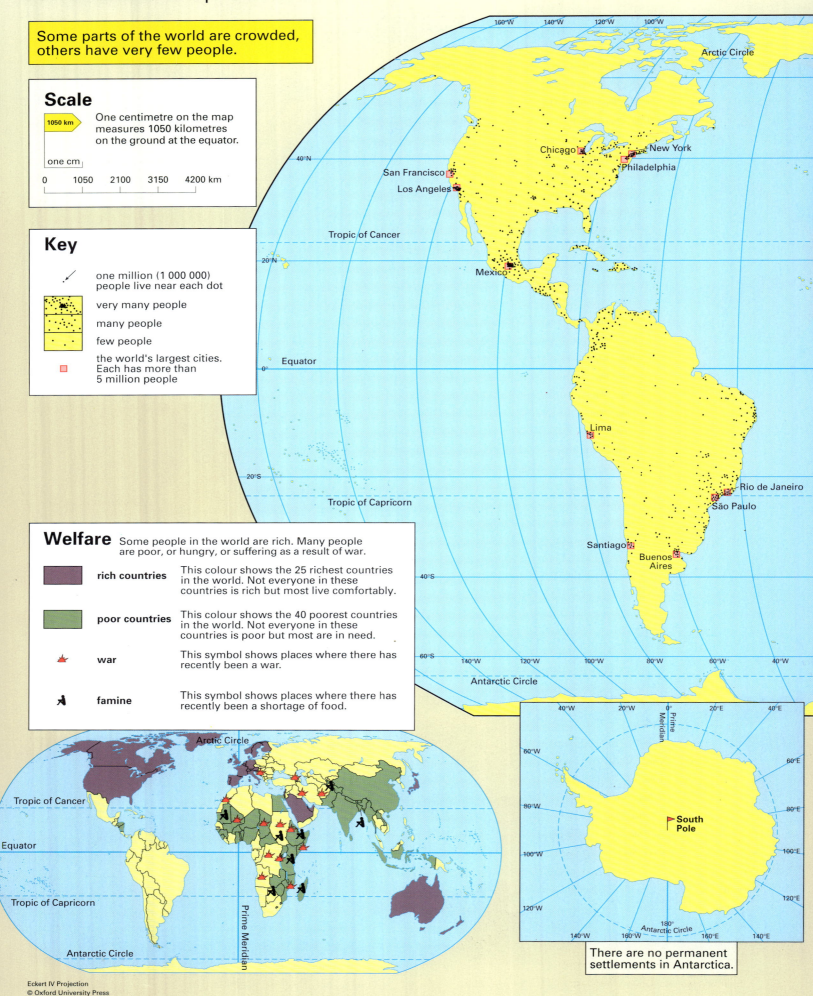

Chicago
New York
Philadelphia
San Francisco
Los Angeles
Mexico
Lima
Rio de Janeiro
São Paulo
Santiago
Buenos Aires

Arctic Circle
Tropic of Cancer
Equator
Tropic of Capricorn
Antarctic Circle

South Pole

There are no permanent settlements in Antarctica.

Arctic Circle
Tropic of Cancer
Equator
Tropic of Capricorn
Antarctic Circle
Prime Meridian

Eckert IV Projection
© Oxford University Press

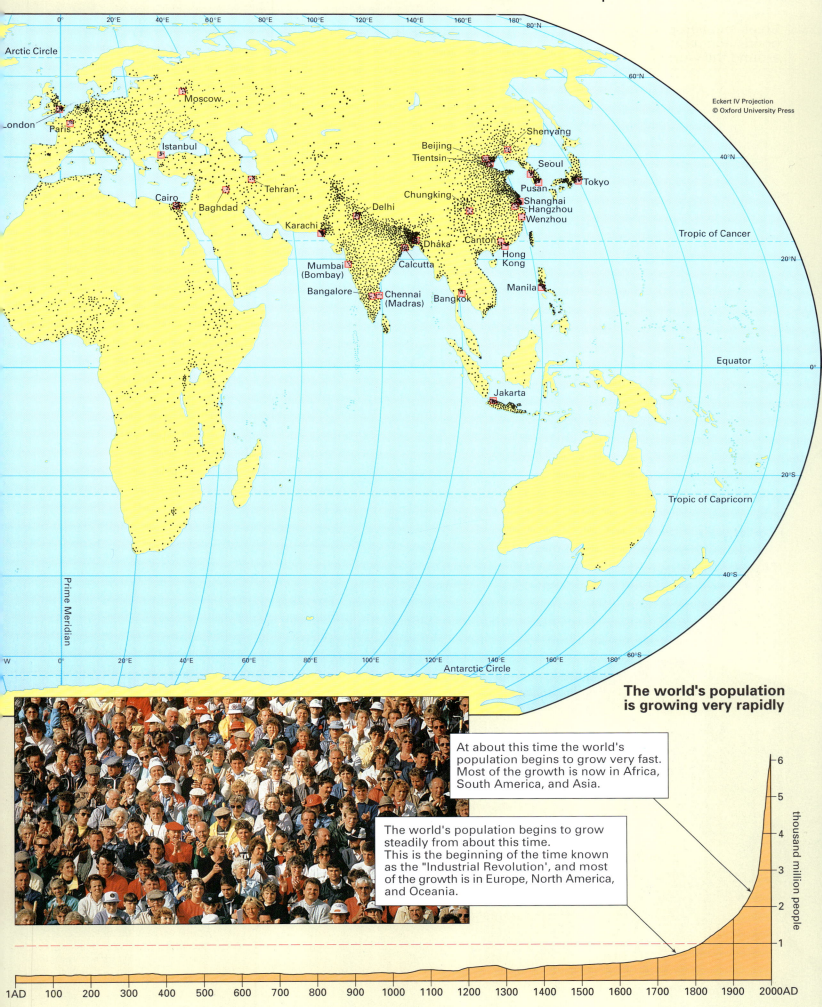

Eckert IV Projection
© Oxford University Press

Arctic Circle

London
Paris
Moscow
Istanbul
Cairo
Baghdad
Tehran
Delhi
Karachi
Mumbai (Bombay)
Bangalore
Chennai (Madras)
Shenyang
Beijing
Tientsin
Seoul
Pusan
Tokyo
Chungking
Shanghai
Hangzhou
Wenzhou
Dhaka
Calcutta
Canton
Hong Kong
Bangkok
Manila
Jakarta

80°N
60°N
40°N
Tropic of Cancer
20°N
Equator 0°
20°S
Tropic of Capricorn
40°S
60°S
Antarctic Circle

Prime Meridian

**The world's population
is growing very rapidly**

At about this time the world's
population begins to grow very fast.
Most of the growth is now in Africa,
South America, and Asia.

The world's population begins to grow
steadily from about this time.
This is the beginning of the time known
as the "Industrial Revolution", and most
of the growth is in Europe, North America,
and Oceania.

thousand million people

6
5
4
3
2
1

1AD 100 200 300 400 500 600 700 800 900 1000 1100 1200 1300 1400 1500 1600 1700 1800 1900 2000AD

Ships and aeroplanes carry goods and passengers around the world.

Anchorage

Victoria

San Francisco

New York

Tokyo

Yokohama

Hong Kong

Honolulu

Antigua

Singapore

Equator

Sydney

Auckland

Los Angeles

Rio de Jan

Buenos Aires

The map shows only the busiest air and sea routes. Many other journeys by aeroplane and ship take place around the world.

Anchorage

North Pole

London

A flight from London to Anchorage passes near the North Pole.

This Boeing 747 takes 10.5 hours to fly from London Heathrow to Antigua.

Gall Projection
© Oxford University Press

London
Hamburg
⊕ Moscow
Kuwait
Mumbai
Lagos
Hong Kong
Tokyo
Yokohama
Honolulu
Singapore
Equator
Sydney
Auckland

This container ship takes 25 days to sail from Hamburg to Buenos Aires.

This oil tanker takes 18 days to sail from Kuwait to the United Kingdom.

Scale

1200 km

One centimetre on the map measures 1200 kilometres on the ground at the Equator.

one cm

0   1200   2400   3600   4800 km

It is about 40 000 kilometres (25 000 miles) around the world.

Key

────── international boundary

────── main shipping lanes

•   major port

        main air routes

⊕   major airport

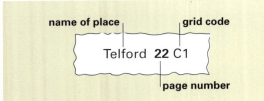

name of place · grid code

Telford **22** C1

page number